18.10

Education and Cultural Pluralism

EDUCATIONAL ANALYSIS

General Editors: Philip Taylor and Colin Richards

CONTEMPORARY ANALYSIS IN EDUCATION SERIES

General Editor: Philip Taylor

Contemporary Analysis in Education Series

Education and Cultural Pluralism

Edited by
Maurice Craft
University of Nottingham

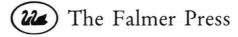 The Falmer Press

(A member of the Taylor & Francis Group)
London and Philadelphia

UK   The Falmer Press, Falmer House, Barcombe, Lewes, East Sussex, BN8 5DL

USA   The Falmer Press, Taylor & Francis Inc., 242 Cherry Street, Philadelphia, PA 19106-1906

First published in 1984

Library of Congress Cataloging in Publication Data

Main entry under title:

Education and cultural pluralism.

   (Contemporary analysis in education series)
   Bibliography: p.
   Includes index.
   Contents: Education for diversity/Maurice Craft—
Policy responses in education/Richard Willey—
Curriculum and assessment/James Lynch—Intercultural
relations in the classroom/Ken Thomas—[etc.].
   1. Minorities—Education—Great Britain—Addresses,
essays, lectures. 2. Education, Bilingual—Great
Britain—Addresses, essays, lectures. 3. Intercultural
education—Great Britain—Addresses, essays, lectures.
4. Pluralism (Social sciences)—Addresses, essays,
lectures. 5. Community and school—Great Britain—
Addresses, essays, lectures. I. Craft, Maurice,
1932-   . II. Series.
LC3736.G6E33   1984   371.97′0941   84-1673
ISBN 0-85000-000-X (pbk.)

Jacket design by Leonard Williams

Typeset in 11/13 Garamond by
by Imago Publishing Ltd., Thame, Oxon.

*Printed in Great Britain by Taylor & Francis (Printers) Ltd,
Basingstoke*

Contents

Editor's Introduction

This collection of papers has two purposes. First, it offers to those wishing to know more about what is meant by 'multicultural education' an introduction to several of its most significant dimensions. It therefore includes chapters which review the development of educational policy, the school curriculum, language issues, intercultural relations in the classroom, the educational performance of West Indian and other ethnic minority children, and the relationships of home, school and community in a diverse society.

But a second aim is to take a little further the analysis of the purposes and the practice of education in a culturally plural society. In as politically sensitive a field as race relations, the discussion of issues in education, as in other areas of social policy such as housing or employment, is particularly subject to the polemics of left and right. The systematic analysis of behaviour and belief becomes more constrained, and the task of those whose role it is to design and to implement policy becomes more difficult in the absence of reliable general guidelines from the academic literature. A second major purpose of this symposium has therefore been to make a contribution to mature reflection, and a polemical treatment has been avoided in favour of a more open appraisal of theory and practice. The several papers consider the policy implications of equality, diversity and social cohesion as societal objectives, the nature and limitations of popular assumptions in multicultural education, the available research evidence and the methodologies used to gather it. Such conclusions as are indicated are — to social scientists — fairly predictable: the issues are complex and have generally been oversimplified, the data are frequently imperfect and incomplete, practice has often been the product of expediency rather than of long-term strategy. Hopefully, the symposium will be helpful to teachers, teacher educators and their students in contributing to the open, systematic and rigorous analysis of a particularly complex and challenging area of educational practice and social policy. Policymakers will also find many indications of areas of need and possible lines of development.

But while seeking to contribute to mature reflection and to avoid polemics, the issue of ideology — a central feature of multicultural education — has not been side-stepped in the following pages. All debate in the field of educability has been characterized by competing interpretations and by ideological conflict; this is no new phenomenon. Indeed, it has frequently helped clarify our understanding of the nature of the problem, and has enriched the range of possible lines of analysis. Only at the point where a single, blinkered view has been assertively pursued has the ideological nature of comment and enquiry proved limiting. Thus, the analysis of home versus school factors in educational performance, the respective roles of teachers and parents and the ways in which they come to be defined, the nature of the curriculum and of what counts as worthwhile knowledge and acceptable language — all have generated a literature in educability which offers a variety of possible interpretations of the role of the school and the status of the pupil. Above all, the issues of power and control, the analysis of what or who determines the shape and functioning of our educational system and to what ends, have been vigorously argued in recent years.

In multicultural education, an aspect of educability which considers avenues of opportunity and equality of access in the same way, the same approaches apply. Do ethnic minority children suffer particular disadvantages at home, or are they subject to unequal treatment at school? Is it the role of teachers to socialize minority pupils into the dominant culture, and of parents to accept and contribute to such a process of assimilation? Is the curriculum unfairly 'loaded' against minority children, and in its valuation of cultural knowledge is it 'racist' in effect? Does the reproduction of a labour force for capitalism asserted by Marxist theorists explain the underachievement of ethnic minority pupils who are being prepared to join a new underclass? These are among the many issues currently argued in multicultural education, and a number are raised in this symposium. They are part of a free academic discourse on the nature of educational disadvantage and of avenues of opportunity, in an open society. But where a single view is asserted, either without supporting empirical data or with the use of crudely conceptualized terms and slogans, we have passed beyond the disciplined exploration of reality into the purveying of ideology.

For some — particularly those responsible for devising effective, practical policies — the increasingly ideological nature of debate in multicultural education is unfortunate, for it is divisive, it inflames opinion in a field in which many tend to react first and reflect afterwards, and it diverts energies from the urgent practical task of building bridges between communities and opening up opportunities for many thousands of individual children and young people. For others, this very viewpoint embodies an ideology of control, and they would argue that a multicultural education which fails to attack social inequality as its prime target is merely acquiescing in the strategies of a 'profoundly racist' society.

My own conviction is that without an unswerving dedication to genuinely open, systematic and rigorous enquiry, we shall not easily achieve equality of opportunity for all our children and the ideal of a tolerant and harmonious society. This means avoiding rhetoric, offering documented argument rather than mere assertion, considering a variety of viewpoints and not merely those which are consistent with this particular ideology or that, and entertaining the possibility that few social phenomena are monocausal. Undoubtedly, a *social class* analysis throws much light upon many aspects of education in any complex society, including ethnically plural societies. Equally, *ethnicity* may help explain numerous aspects of pupil performance or teacher expertise. '*Racism*' may underlie some educational practices and cannot be lightly dismissed. The likelihood, however, of any one of these variables explaining it all is plainly naive. This symposium is therefore devoted to rational analysis in a multidisciplinary field of particular complexity and of singular importance in terms of individual fulfilment and human brotherhood.

Finally, I must gratefully acknowledge the kind invitation of Falmer Press to assemble these papers, the willingness of the contributors to participate and to add to already heavy commitments, the invaluable help of Alma Craft, and the expert assistance of my secretary, Frances Cooper.

Education for Diversity*

Maurice Craft

This opening chapter seeks to locate 'multicultural education' in a broader context; namely, the central dilemma of reconciling education for diversity with provision for a basis of common skills and attitudes.

In education, which is by far the most extensive of the social services, each year sees the rise of fresh enthusiasms: the devizing of new remedies for old problems, the identification of new problems, and the discarding of tried solutions. In recent years, we have had the designation of 'educational priority areas' and a focusing of attention on educational disadvantage;[1] a major report on language policy in schools;[2] detailed national appraisals of the performance of the primary and secondary systems,[3] and of the relationships of the school to its local community;[4] new recommendations on handicapped children;[5] and a continuing discussion of the content and organization of the curriculum.[6] Other significant developments have included a £9 million DES programme on the use of microprocessors in schools; a variety of measures relating to falling school rolls, and to contraction at primary, secondary and tertiary levels; and there has been much discussion of the teaching of shortage subjects.

Multicultural education became the focus of educational debate in 1981, when no less than four major reports on the subject appeared. These were prestigious reports, published, respectively, by the Schools Council,[7] the government-appointed Rampton Committee,[8] the House of Commons Home Affairs Committee,[9]

---

* This chapter is based on *Education for Diversity: The Challenge of Cultural Pluralism*, an inaugural lecture published by the University of Nottingham in 1982, and is reproduced by kind permission of the University.

and Keele University.[10] *The World Yearbook of Education* was devoted to it.[11] That year, the problems of race, erupting in the summer riots, and of the educational implications of a multiracial (or as it is more generally called, a multicultural) society were a predominant theme. A symposium called *Education in the 'Eighties: The Central Issues*, edited by Professors Brian Simon and William Taylor[12] was also published in 1981, and it took the five themes of contraction, work and leisure, equality, our relationship to the European Community, and *race* as being likely to generate fundamental questions for educational policymakers during the coming decade. 1981 ended with Lord Scarman's Report on the Brixton Riots,[13] and again, there was a section on what teachers and teacher trainers might learn from these events.

Since then, there have been the Cockcroft Report on the teaching of mathematics,[14] the Youth Training Scheme, national initiatives in educational management, and a White Paper on teacher education.[15] But in all the flow of practical policy questions in education, we must inevitably look for some pattern, and one perspective is to view education as a social process in which provision relates to the powerful structural and ideological pressures of the wider society. I am thinking here of the changing social and economic structure, and of changing social and political ideologies; those broader currents which lie rather below the surface of everyday events, but which may largely shape the course of educational policy.

One would not deny the role of expediency, an unexpected spark of ingenuity here, a touch of more than average incompetence there; what H.A.L. Fisher might have called 'the interplay of the contingent and the unforeseen'. Educational development has its share of such phenomena. But on the whole, the discussion of educational provision is sterile if we take no account of those social, economic and political factors from which it may have emerged.

The analysis of such variables and of their operation in the changing pattern of educational provision is elusive, nonetheless. For example, the first great waves of New Commonwealth immigration in the 1950s and 1960s led to some special provision for English language teaching in schools but to very little more, for the prevailing ideology at that time was that these children would quickly assimilate and take their place in British society. Twenty years on, the change in social structure is still relatively slight — perhaps 5–6 per cent of the population are members of identifiable ethnic minority groups, possibly reaching 10 per cent by the end of the century — but the prevailing social and political ideology is now no longer so strongly assimilationist in flavour, hence the much greater interest in providing what is called 'multicultural education'.

To take another example, it might well be argued that the twentieth century growth of a huge sector of service industries and professionals stimulated the development of secondary education, and the flow of much greater numbers of young people into GCE and CSE examination courses: a clear response to *structural* change. But the continuing evolution of an egalitarian *political ideology* may have been equally powerful in raising parental aspirations for their children, and encouraging them to stay on to take public examinations. Both structural and ideological variables appear to be operating here.

It is certainly the case that an egalitarian political ideology carried through a reorganization of secondary education along comprehensive lines; and the doctrine of equality of educational opportunity might be thought to have been reflected during the 1960s and 1970s in a range of educational developments: the reform of ability streaming in primary — and to some extent in secondary — education; a concern for closer home-school relations, and for more sophisticated systems of pastoral care and school welfare provision; and a movement for greater accountability in education, including the reform of school governing bodies which is giving the local community a greater say in the running of its schools.

A great deal of the interest in *multicultural education* may be related to a concern for equality of educational opportunity in the same way. More than fifty studies of the school performance of children of New Commonwealth origin, compared with that of white children, have been carried out in Britain since the early 1960s, up to and including that of the Rampton Committee in 1981,[16] and there have been more since then. The underlying assumption, stated explicitly in most cases, has been that comparable schooling outcomes should not only be possible but that they are also profoundly desirable.

Education and Social Continuity: Conformity versus Diversity

I imagine that few would resist the conclusion that educational change almost invariably follows social change, and rarely precedes it; and to my mind, policy recommendations for increasing the scale of resources here or for modifying techniques there can frequently be related to broader developments of a structural or ideological kind —

sometimes representing a national consensus and often the interplay of conflicting pressures of one sort or another.

A further aspect of this question is to say that the greater part of the educational enterprise in any society is likely to be concerned with social continuity rather than social change; with the cultivation of those cognitive, affective and social skills which a society values, and which is achieved not simply through the stated curriculum but also through a 'hidden curriculum' which may convey the concepts of planning, persistence and problem-solving, notions of power and authority, or patterns of social differentiation.[17] We are told that this so-called hidden curriculum may be embodied in the layout of desks or the question and answer techniques of teachers; that this is the way in which the social relationships — and in particular, the social hierarchies — of the marketplace, the factory and of bureaucracy are reproduced from generation to generation.

On the other hand, while schools quite clearly devote much of their efforts to social, economic and political continuity, they do also contribute to *change*. They generate an output of social criticism in each generation, and an element of original thinking across a broad spectrum. It is perhaps too simple an analysis of the social process to argue that education has only a conservative function, and this brings me to the central question with which I am concerned in this paper. To what extent does schooling aim to promote similarity in its clients, and to what extent does it foster individual differences? How far is it concerned simply to reproduce the type rather than allowing for individual growth beyond the type? How important is *education for diversity*?

This must obviously vary according to the parent society. A prevailing social and political ideology which emphasizes conformity is likely to be reflected in school practices which minimize individualized learning; a more liberal regime may do the opposite. All societies strike a balance somewhere along the continuum. Is education regarded primarily as a social or an individual good? Does the educational system generally seek to foster uniformity or to celebrate variety?

In terms of my earlier comments, it seems self-evident that social continuity is likely to be the main aim of all educational systems; but in highly industrialized societies, and particularly in social democracies, continuity includes the capacity to initiate and adapt to change — a paradox. Even so, there will be limits. How far can diversity be pursued before social cohesion is put at risk? Diversity may be preferred to conformity, but without a good measure of agreement there is likely to be social breakdown. As Durkheim put it in his celebrated analysis of social solidarity, societies with a highly developed division of labour do generate an internal interdependence; but without a core of common beliefs and sentiments — a 'collective conscience' — they must disintegrate.

Issues such as these have a long history, with origins in political and social theory and their related disciplines. Here there is an emphasis upon individualism, the essential goodness of man, man as the raw material of society; there we find a more pessimistic view, a greater concern for socialization and social control, and a belief that society comprises more than its constituent members. For Rousseau, 'man is naturally good, and only by institutions is he made bad',[18] and for Spencer the nature of society can only be explained by 'the nature of its component individuals'.[19] But quite opposite views were held by Hobbes for whom life in a state of nature is a war of all against all, 'nasty, brutish and short',[20] and by Comte who claimed that 'society is no more decomposable into individuals than a geometric surface is into lines, or a line into points'.[21]

But the antithesis of individual and society is, of course, artificial and unrealistic. While society may be more than a collection of individuals, individuals are only fully human as members of society. Even Durkheim, who argued that the properties of groups are independent of the characteristics of their individual members, came to believe that social control operates from both outside and within individuals; that external moral obligations also become internalized, that in this sense society is, as he put it, 'something beyond us and something in ourselves'.[22]

Echoes of this ancient disputation about the relationship of the individual and society appear, as we might expect, in the philosophy of education, and consequently in discussions about the school curriculum and educational policymaking. Those who have argued that the word 'education' derives from *educare* — to train or to mould — have been opposed by those who prefer *educere* — to lead out. The former, in the tradition of Hobbes and Durkheim, have stressed social conformity, the reproduction of the type, and a curriculum emphasizing instruction, obedience and the acquisition of knowledge. The latter, who represent the child-centred tradition, following Rousseau or Froebel, have preferred self-expression, individual curiosity and creativity, and a curriculum embodying choice.

Again, these are 'ideal types' (or models), and reality lies somewhere between them. The education of the individual implies the existence of society. The identification and definition of a child's inner resources is socially derived; and as Professor Peters has put it, 'the "potentialities" of the individual can only be developed within the framework of some socially structured pursuit into which he has to be initiated'.[23]

Educational planning must obviously take account of both the individual *and* societal aspects of the equation, and the balance which is struck will vary from place to place as it has from time to time in our own society. The closing decades of the last century, for example, found Britain with a newly extended franchise, facing increased economic and military competition from the rising powers of Europe, North America and the Far East. No surprise then that W. E. Forster, in introducing the 1870 Education Act, which greatly extended elementary schooling, concluded his speech: 'Upon the speedy provision of elementary education depends our individual prosperity . . . the good, the safe working of our constitutional system . . . [and] also our national power.'[24] No mention here of individual needs. Not much in the Spens Report either, some seventy years later, in 1938:

> Speaking broadly, the interest of the State is to see that the schools provide the means by which the nation's life may be maintained in its integrity from generation to generation . . . there is the unformulated but very real demand of the community that the young shall grow up in conformity with the national ethos.[25]

But twenty years on, by 1959, the Crowther Report was reflecting the balance of individual and societal needs. Crowther regarded education as a *human right*, one of the social services to be provided by the welfare state, and provided — as the Report put it — 'regardless of whether, in each individual case, there will be any return'. But education, it argued, is also a *national investment*, and while — as the Report said — 'primacy must be given to the human rights of the individual boy or girl . . . we do not believe that the pursuit of national efficiency can be ranked much lower — not least because without it the human rights themselves will not be secure'.[26] Even the Robbins Report, which certainly regarded education as an investment in a nation's future, argued that 'the goal is not productivity as such but the good life that productivity makes possible'.[27]

The 1977 Green Paper, as many will recall, reflected an unease about the responsiveness of the educational system to national economic needs. But even this Report placed first in a list of educational aims, 'to help children develop lively, enquiring minds',[28] and this objective was carried through into the 1981 DES curriculum document[29] which summarized the current orthodoxy as follows: 'Since school education prepares the child for adult life, the way in which the school helps him develop his potential must also be related to his subsequent needs and responsibilites as an active member of our society' (para. 3). Quite a subtle blend.

Education, Industrialization and Social Democracy

So far, I have argued that education may be viewed as a process devoted largely to ensuring social continuity, but also to engendering social change — a process linked to broader structural and ideological variables, and varying with time and place according to the emphasis which is placed upon the development of the *individual* as compared with the interests of *society*. I have recalled the reflections of social theorists, educational philosophers and educational policymakers upon this fundamental — and essentially political — question; and I have noted that while the dichotomy is an unreal one, and that education is generally felt to be both a social and an individual good, the balance does vary from time to time and place to place.

For me, as I have already suggested, the most interesting aspect of the dichotomy at the present time is the extent to which we are educating for diversity rather than for social cohesion, and this is bound to be a central dilemma in a society such as our own which is *highly industrialized, democratic*, and *culturally plural*. Let us take each of these in turn.

A *highly industrialized* society requiring many thousands of different skills, characterized by constant technological change (and therefore social change), and with a national labour market, requires an educational system which can generate a wide range of competencies, the capacity to adapt to change (but also to contribute to it), and the willingness to be geographically and socially mobile. Our schools therefore foster individualized learning: individual assignments in the primary school; and a wide range of options at secondary level, with an increasingly sophisticated system of guidance and counselling to help match individual interests and aptitudes to a complex range of opportunities. Individual creativity, whether in writing, the arts curriculum, the sciences, or PE, is encouraged. Great stress is placed on individual assessment and individual achievement, institutionalized through a massive system of public examinations.

But the national requirement for similarity as well as difference

remains: much teaching is class and group teaching; we have uni-
forms, and school assemblies. In recent years there has been a strong
movement towards an agreed core curriculum, and away from what
have come to be regarded as over-extended option systems offering
an excessive range of choice and early specialization. Central government has taken a firmer hold on the curriculum, hitherto regarded as
the province of LEAs, schools and individual teachers, and an
Assessment of Performance Unit has been established by the DES to
monitor standards in basic subjects. Industry, too, has expressed
interest in the schools maintaining a broad curriculum for all,
allowing for greater flexibility in the work situation. And there is no
shortage of critics who claim that even the seemingly most individualized learning strategies still embody powerful systems of control.

The second of my three categories, *social democracy*, no less than
industrialization, sets the schools a problem in balancing education
for diversity with education for conformity. The essence of our
political ethic is respect for persons, regarding each individual as an
end in himself; and a great part of British schooling is concerned with
the cultivation of individual judgement, the fullest development of an
individual's abilities, a willingness to accept personal responsibility
for personal decisions. Few attributes, in fact, are rewarded as highly
as an independent critical capacity in our educational system. If
originality is out of reach, an informed scepticism will do.

Set against this there are all the devices traditionally used to
cultivate team spirit, school pride, corporate responsibility. Non-
conformity is only tolerated within the limits set by existing codes
and established hierarchies. Independent critical judgement has always to be informed by an awareness of existing orthodoxies. This is
individualism within a social context. For Mannheim, education in a
democratic society offers 'equal attention ... to the spontaneity of a
person and to the significance of the environment in which this
person grows'.[30]

Education and Cultural Pluralism

However, it is when we come to consider the third characteristic,
cultural pluralism, the mosaic of norms and values contained in a
single society, that the tension between conformity and diversity in
education is at its greatest.

A society possessing a relatively homogeneous culture, with
little variation of belief or practice, is likely to share the universal

concern for social continuity which I have sought to describe. If that society is industrialized and democratic, it may also have a commitment to social change. Its schools may seek to convey standards of accomplishment, ingenuity, diligence and sincerity beyond those to be found in the homes, offices and factories in the streets outside. But where a society has a more *heterogeneous* culture, and those streets contain a variety of family types, religious and moral codes, even spoken languages, what then? Is the school to make provision for all these variations? Or should it ignore them, and concentrate on its more conservative function, and seek assimilation?

The interesting thing is that it is quite difficult to find an example of a relatively homogeneous culture. Virtually all societies are culturally plural. Many have *religious* variations: they may be predominantly Roman Catholic, with Protestant and other minorities; Protestant, with Roman Catholic and Jewish minorities; Jewish, with Muslim and Christian minorities; Muslim, with Hindu and Christian minorities. All but the very smallest have *regional* variations: urban/rural, small town/large city, highland/lowland. Most industrialized societies have subcultures based on *age*: who will deny the reality of a distinctive adolescent subculture, for example, in complex societies like our own? Indeed, the rate of technological and social change is now so great that intergenerational differences of all kinds have come into existence. All such societies are stratified by *social class*, with distinctive life-styles and life-chances; and many are vertically divided by *ethnicity*, a sense of peoplehood, which may even be rigidified into impermeable caste divisions. A recent survey has identified no less than seventy-three such ethnic groups in Europe, on the basis of a distinctive culture, language, consciousness, and sometimes a distinctive political status and territory too.[31] The Basques, Flemings and Lapps are merely the most well-known of them. Another survey has located *862* ethnic groups in the world as a whole.[32] Indeed, according to Connor (1972), only twelve out of 132 independent states in 1971 could be considered ethnically homogeneous.[33]

Cultural pluralism in Britain has existed for quite some time, centuries in fact; but it has become more widely recognized with growing egalitarianism, and with the greater acceptance of individual autonomy in all aspects of behaviour and belief. The greater informality in dress and social relationships generally, the use of regional accents on radio and television, the rise of Welsh and Scottish nationalism, these are among the more obvious examples which reflect these ideological changes. Structural changes, such as social mobility, the continuing population drift from north to south, and New Commonwealth immigration must also have contributed to a growing recognition and acceptance of cultural pluralism in Britain.

There have also been worldwide expressions of ethnicity, the greater awareness of cultural identity and cultural traditions — a so-called 'ethnic revival' — and there is no reason to suppose that Britain has been immune to these global trends. The long-standing inter-ethnic conflict in Northern Ireland continues, and it has been paralleled on every continent: Quebec, Cyprus, Central Africa, and more recently, Sri Lanka.

In education, cultural pluralism has always been recognized to some extent. So far as *religious* differences are concerned, the right of parents of withdraw their children from morning assembly or RE lessons, or to place them in specifically denominational schools, has existed for many years. The *community* education movement has been associated with rural reconstruction, as well as with the special needs of inner urban districts and suburban overspill estates — a recognition of locality differences. The appointment of parent governors, and the proposals for devizing school curricula which are more closely related to local social conditions are the most recent forms of this kind of pluralism in education. And we should not forget that some schools in Wales have long since taught through the medium of Welsh, where that is the local spoken language.

As to *age-related* subcultures, schools everywhere are age-specific, a recognition of special needs which we take completely for granted. Indeed, until recently, *tripartite secondary education* was taken for granted, a nation-wide system based on the distinctive needs of what were felt to be three broad 'types' of adolescent identified by educational psychologists and enshrined in the Hadow, Spens and Norwood Reports of forty and fifty years ago. That form of education for diversity was eventually found unacceptable for it was felt to limit life-chances for too many children, and to maintain impermeable social class subcultures. The diversity offered by tripartite secondary education was too crudely formulated, and post-war egalitarianism sought *more equal* opportunities of becoming unequal. It might also be thought to have failed to provide an adequate flow of talent for an expanding economy.

The pendulum thus swung away from diversity in secondary education towards the common secondary school. 'Comprehensive reorganization' was ideologically and structurally more in tune with social needs, and seemed to offer promise of greater social cohesion. But the antithesis of cohesion and diversity remained, and the common secondary school in turn generated elaborate *internal* provision for the varied needs of its pupils — through banding, streaming and grouping, and extensive programmes of options. These developments, it will be recalled, were accompanied during the 1970s by the proposals of Bantock and of Midwinter for distinctive styles of education for working-class children;[34] and these, in turn, were followed by proposals such as those of Lawton for a 'common culture' curriculum followed by *all* children, but allowing for differing levels of achievement.[35]

A great deal of this recent history therefore seems to reflect the continuing attempts of the educational system to cater for cultural pluralism; and in particular, to strike an acceptable balance between educating for difference and educating for similarity, for diversity and also for consensus.

Education and Social Class

Social class has been an important part of the debate because class forms a basic aspect of cultural pluralism in British society; and as I have tried to indicate, because of the continuing concern to equalize educational opportunity. The controversy over what, in the 1960s and 1970s was called 'cultural deprivation' is a useful illustration.

In trying to explain the persistence of working-class under-achievement in primary and secondary schools, many theorists argued that these children were suffering from 'culture clash'. The language, ethos and life-experience of schools and teachers were said to be so different from those of their working-class pupils as to put them at a considerable disadvantage. They were, it was said, 'culturally deprived', and they needed compensatory education to make up for their deficiencies. Others have since claimed that such children are different rather than deficient. And some have talked in terms of *biculturalism*, suggesting, for example, that working-class children be educated in standard English and in the value orientations of school; but that they should also be encouraged to make use of their own dialect and life experience, and take pride in them.

In terms of the antithesis of diversity and conformity, this example seems to typify the argument. On the one hand, we may hold that all cultures — working class/middle class, urban/rural, Roman Catholic/Protestant — have *intrinsic validity*, and embody an intricate and often distinctive network of norms, values and traditions. A social democracy, committed to liberty and equality, is committed to diversity; and our schools have a prime responsibility to recognize and to further it.

On the other hand, in the interests of social cohesion and the survival of society, we may argue that children possessing varying home cultures must also be helped to acquire linguistic, cognitive and social skills of broader value. Indeed, without such skills they will be at a considerable handicap in education, and in the occupational and other opportunities linked to educational achievement. 'Different' or 'deficient', they must not be disadvantaged. In this sense, education for conformity in a social democracy is the means to the fullest exploitation of diversity.

The *challenge* of cultural pluralism is that in each generation we have to update our knowledge of the diversity within our society, incorporating this into our educational provision. Secondly, we have to reach agreement about the nature of educating for conformity, and this is more than simply a pedagogical task, it is essentially political. The dominant culture — be it middle-class, Protestant, or whatever — is likely to be taken as the norm to which members of other cultures must conform; lip service may be paid to the notion of an intercultural 'melting pot', but this is rarely the reality. For educationalists, the problem is to decide upon the *minimum* level of acculturation necessary for full participation in society, and the *maximum* extent to which diversity might be encouraged.

Education and Ethnicity

So far, I have argued that cultural pluralism sets the sternest tests for our political ideals in presenting a tension between education for diversity, and education for consensus. I have suggested that few societies are culturally homogeneous, and that social class is a predominant source of pluralism almost everywhere. But as I indicated earlier, we frequently find vertical social divisions too, the pluralism of *ethnicity*: a sense of peoplehood, of cohesive traditions, usually with distinctive religious and linguistic characteristics, sometimes with a regional basis, but almost always cutting across the horizontal stratification of age and social class.

Ethnic variations have always existed in Britain. Apart from the Scots and Welsh, and the various English tribes of earlier times, there have been Irish and Jews in Britain since the Middle Ages, and black people since at least the sixteenth century. As I suggested earlier, migration and changes in the climate of opinion here and abroad are among the factors which have led to the fuller recognition of ethnic and other forms of pluralism in more recent times.

But of all forms of cultural pluralism, it is *ethnicity* which currently offers the greatest challenge, for migration from overseas has undoubtedly added greater cultural variety than can be found, say, in the spectrum of social class. There is consequently a rather greater concern about social cohesion, and a sharper debate about the balance of diversity and conformity.

Nonetheless, it is worth recalling some of the past principles and practices of cultural pluralism in British education, in the new context of greater ethnic variety. We already recognize differences relating to pupil age, religion and language in many of our schools and teacher training institutions. We allow for locality differences through school governing bodies. Tripartite secondary education was structured on a premise (specious though it proved to be) of aptitude difference. Awareness of class-related variations in language code, upbringing and perception is now part of the professional equipment of all young teachers.

Ethnic variations are no different in kind, for they include religion, language, community participation, and family background. The issues relating to conformity are also very similar: comprehensive reorganization replaced separatism by a common secondary school with the aim of providing both a better basis of social cohesion and greater individual opportunity. The debate about class differences in education has been much concerned with the question of *which* culture working-class children should be required to assimilate to, and with the ethics and practicality of biculturalism and bidialectalism. All this can be precisely paralleled in terms of the education of ethnic minority children, but the issues are more sharply defined and the dilemmas more tantalizing.

Multicultural Education

First, let us be clear about the scale of the question. As I indicated earlier, perhaps three million British residents belong to identifiable ethnic minorities, of whom a large and increasing proportion were born here. They cover a very wide range: well over half a million from Germany, Poland, Italy, Spain and elsewhere in Europe; perhaps one million from the West Indies, India and Pakistan; and about one-third of a million from New Commonwealth territories in Africa, the Mediterranean and the Far East. These figures exclude

700,000 people born in the Irish Republic, and some 400,000 Jews mostly born here.[36]

The overall figure of around 5–6 per cent of Britain's total population is very small compared, say, with that of Australia where some 20 per cent of the population are from non-English speaking overseas cultures.[37] On the other hand, this 5–6 per cent is not evenly distributed. Chain migration and the availability of work and cheap accommodation have attracted newcomers to the urban centres and particularly to Greater London and the West Midlands, where the proportions may be much greater. At the 1971 Census, for example, 15 per cent of the population of Islington North (in London) were born in the New Commonwealth, and 6 per cent in Ireland; while in Birmingham, 20 per cent of the population of Ladywood were from the New Commonwealth. Individual localities may have much greater percentages.[38]

But while not evenly spread, ethnic minority communities now exist in many parts of Britain. The Maltese live mainly in London, but communities of 200 or more exist in half-a-dozen cities; the Chinese are mainly in London and Liverpool, but small communities may be found in more than twenty other urban centres from Plymouth to Edinburgh; while the Cypriots are spread yet more evenly from Brighton to Glasgow. Outside London, there are communities of 1000 or more Italians in six British cities, and of Poles in nine or ten.[39]

The educational implications of these random figures would seem to be two-fold: first, that ethnic diversity has created particular needs in many primary and secondary schools in urban areas where there are sizeable minority communities; and second, that the national spread of ethnic minorities means that all children are going to encounter them in adult life, if not before, and that they therefore need fuller preparation for growing up in a multicultural society. Let us take each in turn.

The Particular Needs of Ethnic Minority Children

The particular needs of ethnic minority children may be illustrated by the Inner London Education Authority's language surveys. The report published in December 1981 showed that 14 per cent of all the Authority's children (some 45,000) speak a tongue other than English outside the classroom — 131 different languages in all, headed by Bengali, Turkish and Greek.[40] Nor is linguistic diversity restricted to the metropolis. Current research at London University shows that 27 per cent of Peterborough's primary school population, for example, have some competence in forty-three languages other than English, principally Punjabi and Italian[41]. (Some of this material is discussed in this volume; see Linguistic Minorities Project, pp. 95–116.)

Apart from the loss of a valuable national resource if linguistic talents of this kind are allowed to dissipate, it may also be the case that the education of such children will be retarded if their fluency in the mother tongue is not utilized by teachers. Furthermore, it may be argued that to individual community groups the loss of the mother tongue will weaken the mother culture, including religious faith. This in turn may give rise to intergenerational stresses within the family; and, most serious of all, to a loss of *identity* in a society in which full acceptance of ethnic minorities is not always readily accorded. Culture maintenance is important.

As the Bullock Report, an authoritative statement on language in education put it in a widely celebrated comment: '... No child should be expected to cast off the language and culture of the home as he crosses the school threshold'.[42] There is therefore rising pressure for mother tongue teaching, and for some extension of O- and A-level programmes in modern languages to take account of the needs particularly of Asian pupils, languages which are at present largely taught outside mainstream education in evening and weekend supplementary schools. There is also some pressure for separate schooling for Sikh and Muslim children. As we have seen, there are precedents for all these kinds of provision in our educational system, and given our traditional commitment to education for diversity the case has been made. There are, of course, logistical questions: are the specialist teachers available, and is there yet any national provision for training them?[43] Will there be viable teaching groups anywhere outside the main centres of non-English speaking minority communities?

Then there are the more difficult aspects of education for diversity in an ethnically plural society. What mother tongue is to be taught in each case: a standard version? Or the regional dialect used by the particular minority community? Secondly, mother tongue is probably best taught alongside mother culture, just as we have traditionally taught French language together with French literature and civilization. But what *is* the mother culture of Pakistani children born and brought up in Preston or Italians raised in Bedford? The cultural traditions of these minority communities may well be distinctive, and many children may be partially or even fully bilingual. But such communities are unlikely to have the more hierarchical, sexist and rural characteristics of the regions of origin. These are questions for minority group leaders as much as for educationalists.

As I have argued, education for diversity is always paralleled by education for social cohesion. Until recently, this has meant the provision of special tuition in English as a second language, and continuing language support across the curriculum for ethnic minority children; little more. With the greater recognition and acceptance of cultural pluralism, a frankly assimilationist policy has moved more in the direction of *biculturalism*: equipping minority group children with the language and other skills essential for living in modern Britain, but nonetheless, recognizing, accepting, respecting, and encouraging the development of other cultural forms brought into school by them.

This, of course, precisely parallels the earlier suggestions of a bicultural approach to the education of children of diverse social class backgrounds.

Now, in talking about the particular needs of minority children (as compared with the educational needs of all children) in an ethnically plural society, I have taken children from non-English speaking homes as presenting the clearest examples of the problems and opportunities which arise. But very similar issues arise with West Indian school children who do speak English and were mostly born here. Creole dialects may retard school progress unless they are used as a *resource* by teachers. These dialects, like the Asian, African and European languages of other ethnic minority children, offer the same link with cultural traditions and provide the same basis of communal pride.

This diversity, I would contend, is again a valuable community asset, for it may engender self-respect and a sense of identity in what, for all of us who live in large-scale and complex industrial societies, is an increasingly stressful and alienating social environment. But as with the debates about working-class and regional dialects, West Indian children clearly require a capacity to speak and write fluently in standard English; they must be *bidialectal*, and adding to the child's language repertoire in this way may provide the necessary basis both for social cohesion and for equality of opportunity for individual achievement.

So much for a few brief remarks on the particular needs of ethnic minority children. It will, I think, be clear that the blending of diversity and uniformity, reproducing the type but allowing for differentiation, raises all the familiar issues (but more sharply) than in the case of religious, regional and social class differences. At the policy level the debates have been at least as fierce. Within the profession, the initial and in-service training of teachers have been slow to respond; and at the level of classroom practice and school organization, the many opportunities have yet to be fully grasped.

The Needs of All Children in a Multicultural Society

When we come to the second category, what education should be offering *all* children in a multicultural society, as distinct from the particular needs of minority group children, the difficulties are just as great but the opportunities just as attractive. If we are concerned about tolerance and social harmony, about the reduction of conflict and the building of bridges, there are clear implications for the curriculum, for staffing, and for books and materials. On the face of it, this is an argument for *social cohesion*, and indeed it is. But by learning more about and paying greater respect to minority cultures (and by learning more about the varied origins of the *majority* culture), we are in fact cultivating an intelligent appreciation of *diversity*.

As I mentioned earlier, proposals for a 'common culture' curriculum have attracted a good deal of attention during the past decade, seeking to provide a balanced programme for all children up to the age of 16. It has been argued that exposure to perspectives such as the mathematical, the scientific, the linguistic or the social and political are essential for all children — not just the most able who formerly attended grammar schools. Differentiation should come through the level of individual achievement in each of these areas, and not through streaming between or within schools. So while allowing for diversity, this is an argument for consensus in a class stratified society.

If we now take account of cultural pluralism, we need to add no new elements to the common culture curriculum for all children, but simply a greater *awareness* of pluralism. For example, work in the humanities would take fuller account of the variety of minority cultures in modern Britain, underscoring their intrinsic worth; sometimes including examples of minority literature, art, music, drama; and extending the range of modern language and RE teaching — for the benefit of *all* pupils. Schoolwork in history, but also in science, mathematics and religion could hardly avoid reference to the diverse origins of European civilization. A more conscious effort would be made to highlight the cultural assumptions and ethnocentric perspectives of each area of the curriculum.

Now many teachers have been aware for some time past of the

need to make more explicit the overseas origins of British culture; to counter ethnocentrism, prejudice and even racism in their work with all children. The avoidance of history textbooks presenting a blatantly one-sided view of world events; or of syllabuses which only reflect European literature, religions, exploration, art or scientific discovery, is not new. But nor is it as basic an aspect of professional competence as one might expect in the 1980s, and this is something which is now undergoing urgent review by teacher trainers.[44]

The opportunities for enriching the curriculum for *all* children thus seem almost limitless, although the road is not always an easy one. What is one to do, for example, about the social, national, sexual or ethnic stereotypes to be found in school books and other materials? Are Shakespeare's *Merchant of Venice*, Defoe's *Robinson Crusoe* or Dickens' *Oliver Twist* to be excluded? Should the class snobbery of P.G. Wodehouse, the jingoism of Kipling, or the sexism of Scott Fitzgerald be rendered suspect? A slippery path!

The point, perhaps, is that nothing should be taught unthinkingly and uncritically; cultural assumptions can be placed in their social and historical context, and ethnic or racial stereotypes can provide a basis for open discussion, just as dialect variation can be a rich source in the teaching of English. While some materials may need to be brought up to date, the case is less one of censorship than for the exercise of a more sophisticated level of professional skill.

A common culture curriculum of this kind is for *all* children in a multicultural society. As I have said, those from the majority culture will meet and work with, during their lifetimes, members of ethnic minorities — most of whom were born here. What can be more important than that these relationships are based on mutual understanding and respect, whether children have grown up in the Cotswolds or in Coventry, in the all-white areas of rural England or the more cosmopolitan streets of the conurbations.

They will also be continually in contact, through the mass media, with peoples overseas, in a world which is more interdependent than ever; and the cultivation of a greater understanding of this interdependence, and of a greater respect and tolerance for other ways of life is a further dimension of the question.

Conclusion

In this paper I have sought to argue that education may be viewed not simply as pupils and teachers, classrooms and textbooks, but as a process devoted mainly to providing for social continuity and also to engendering social change. I have suggested that this process is linked to powerful structural and ideological variables in the wider society; and that it may vary according to the importance placed upon *individual development* compared with the perceived needs of *society*. Both are important, indeed, they are inseparable; we have it on good authority, as well as from the evidence of our senses. But a particularly interesting aspect of this dichotomy is the way all educational systems must strike a balance between educating for variety and educating for conformity, providing for difference and for similarity, ensuring diversity but also cohesion.

I have noted that diversity is more likely to be pursued in complex, industrial societies; and that social democracies in particular will foster it. But it is *cultural pluralism* — especially ethnicity — which produces the greatest tension between educating for diversity and educating for consensus; for not only is a plural society, by definition, more diverse, but it also has both a greater need for conformity and a greater natural resistance to it.

Here in Britain, educationalists have to address themselves to both tasks: the celebration of this enriching new diversity, and the conveying of a core of common beliefs and sentiments (Durkheim's 'collective conscience'). This represents a substantial challenge. For educationalists have to decide at what point the acculturation necessary for full participation in society becomes a repressive assimilation; and at what point the celebration of diversity ceases to enrich and becomes potentially divisive. Only a free society gives rise to such excruciatingly difficult problems of educational theory and practice. But I imagine that few of us would have it otherwise.

Notes

1 DES (1972) *Educational Priority: EPA Problems and Policies* ('Halsey Report'), London, HMSO.
2 DES (1975) *A Language for Life* ('Bullock Report'), London, HMSO.
3 DES (1981) *Primary Education in England*, London, HMSO; DES (1979) *Aspects of Secondary Education in England*, London, HMSO.
4 DES (1977) *A New Partnership for Our Schools* ('Taylor Report'), London, HMSO.
5 DES (1978) *Special Educational Needs* ('Warnock Report'), London, HMSO.
6 See, for example, DES (1981) *The School Curriculum*, London, HMSO.
7 SCHOOLS COUNCIL (1981) *Multi-Ethnic Education: The Way Forward* ('Little-Willey Report'), London, Schools Council.

8   DES (1981) *West Indian Children in Our Schools* ('Rampton Report'), London, HMSO.
9   HOUSE OF COMMONS (1981) *Racial Disadvantage*, 5th Report of the Home Affairs Committee, London, HMSO.
10   EGGLESTON, S.J. *et al.* (1981) *In-Service Teacher Education in a Multiracial Society*, University of Keele.
11   MEGARRY, J. *et al.* (Eds) (1981) *Education of Minorities*, London, Kogan Page.
12   SIMON, B. and TAYLOR, W. (Eds) (1981) *Education in the 'Eighties: The Central Issues*, London, Batsford.
13   HOME OFFICE (1981) *The Brixton Disorders* ('Scarman Report'), London, HMSO.
14   DES (1982) *Mathematics Counts* ('Cockcroft Report'), London, HMSO.
15   DES (1983) *Teaching Quality*, London, HMSO.
16   TOMLINSON, S. (1980), 'The educational performance of ethnic minority children', *New Community*, 8, 3, pp. 213–34.
17   See, for example, HARGREAVES, D. (1978), 'Power and the paracurriculum', in RICHARDS, C. (Ed.), *Power and the Curriculum*, Driffield, Nafferton Books.
18   In his essay, 'A Discourse on Inequality' (1754).
19   SPENCER, H. (1891), *The Study of Sociology*, New York, Appleton, p. 52.
20   *Leviathan* (1651).
21   In his *Système de Politique Positive* (1912). Vol. 2, Paris, Crès, p. 181.
22   DURKHEIM, E. (1953) *Sociology and Philosophy*, New York, The Free Press, p. 55.
23   PETERS, R.S. (1966) *Ethics and Education*, London, Allen and Unwin, p. 56.
24   Quoted in MACLURE, J.S. (1979) *Educational Documents*, 4th ed., London, Methuen, pp. 104–5.
25   Quoted in OTTOWAY, A.K.C. (1957) *Education and Society*, London, Routledge, p. 9.
26   MINISTRY OF EDUCATION (1959) *15 to 18* ('Crowther Report'), London, HMSO, paras 83–6.
27   COMMITTEE ON HIGHER EDUCATION (1963) *Higher Education* ('Robbins Report'), London, HMSO, para. 621.
28   DES (1977) *Education in Schools: A Consultative Document*, London, HMSO, para. 1.19.
29   DES (1981) *The School Curriculum*, London, HMSO.
30   MANNHEIM, K. and STEWART, W.A.C. (1962) *An Introduction to the Sociology of Education*, London, Routledge, p. 49.
31   KREJCI, J. and VELIMSKY, V. (1981) *Ethnic and Political Nations in Europe*, London, Croom Helm, p. 48.
32   SAID, A.A. and SIMMONS, L.R. (Eds) (1976) *Ethnicity in an International Context*, New Brunswick, N.J., Transaction Books.
33   CONNOR, W. (1972) 'Nation-building or nation-destroying', *World Politics*, 24, pp. 319–55.
34   See, for example, their contributions to HOOPER, R. (Ed.) (1971) *The*

Curriculum: Context, Design and Development, Edinburgh, Oliver and Boyd.

35 LAWTON, D. (1975) *Class, Culture and the Curriculum*, London, Routledge.

36 Census data reported in: CAMPBELL-PLATT, K. (1978) *Linguistic Minorities in Britain*, London, Runnymede Trust; COMMISSION FOR RACIAL EQUALITY (1979) *Ethnic Minorities in Britain: Statistical Background*, London, CRE; RUNNYMEDE TRUST (1980) *Britain's Black Population*, London, Heinemann; HOME OFFICE RESEARCH UNIT (1981) *Ethnic Minorities in Britain*, London, HMSO.

37 BULLIVANT, B. (1981) *The Pluralist Dilemma in Education*, Sydney, Allen and Unwin.

38 Census data, *op. cit.*

39 *Ibid.*

40 ILEA (1981) *1981 Language Survey* (cyclostyled), ILEA.

41 DR VERITY KHAN's Linguistic Minorities Project at the London University Institute of Education.

42 DES (1975) *A Language for Life* ('Bullock Report'), London, HMSO, para. 20.5.

43 CRAFT, M. and ATKINS, M.J. (1983) *Training Teachers of Ethnic Minority Community Languages*, University of Nottingham.

44 CRAFT, M. (Ed.) (1981) *Teaching in a Multicultural Society: The Task for Teacher Education*, Lewes, Falmer Press.

Policy Responses in Education

Richard Willey

The changing policies of central government, local education author-
ities and individual schools towards the more complex needs of a
plural society are briefly outlined in this review by Dr Willey.

The educational response to cultural diversity has changed markedly
over the last twenty years. There has been a fundamental redefinition
of objectives. Early assimilationist assumptions have been replaced by
'multicultural', pluralist aims. This has major implications for the
development of policies at national, local education authority, and
school levels. Preoccupation with fitting minority ethnic group
children into the existing education system has broadened into
consideration of the implications of cultural diversity for the educational process as a whole. 'Multicultural education' is coming to be
regarded not as a set of disparate and optional extras, but as an
integral part of good education for all children in a society prepared
to accord positive recognition to cultural diversity.

The Development of Multicultural Objectives

Early educational responses to the presence of minority ethnic group
pupils were developed in the context of the broadly assimilationist
approach which government adopted towards post-war immigration.
The policy was assumed rather than explicitly stated. Government
took a largely laissez-faire attitude (Rose, 1969); the newcomers
would simply be absorbed into the majority society, no particular
social policy response was necessary, any difficulties would, given
time and goodwill, take care of themselves. Only slowly was it
recognized that positive initiatives were necessary to counter racial
discrimination in society, and to assess and meet the particular needs

27

of minority ethnic group pupils. Only gradually did a multicultural pluralist definition of aims emerge in which the changed ethnic composition of society was recognized to have implications for members of that society as a whole.

The DES in its first formal advice to LEAs in 1963 was cautious about objectives. '... the extent to which adjustment demands conformity, the kind of conformity that a too narrow interpretation of "integration" would seek to impose, is a matter for rather more careful deliberation than it sometimes receives' (DES, 1963). But two years later, when the Department was recommending dispersal of minority ethnic group children, the premise was categorically assimilationist. In what appears to have been a panic reaction to local difficulties in Southall in London, the DES told authorities, 'As the proportion of immigrant children increases, the problems will become more difficult to solve and the chances of assimilation more remote...' (DES, 1965). At a time of increasing consciousness of negative racial attitudes among the white majority (this was the year in which the first Race Relations Act was introduced), the Department was looking over its shoulder at the response of white parents and the spectre of the 'white backlash'. A sentence placed in italics in the 1965 Circular warned, 'It will be helpful if the parents of non-immigrant children can see that practical measures have been taken to deal with the problems in the schools, and that the progress of their own children is not being restricted by the undue preoccupation of the teaching staff with the linguistic and other difficulties of the immigrant children.' Immigrants *per se* were being identified as constituting a problem, not the specific educational difficulties of some minority ethnic group children.

When the DES next issued advice to authorities in 1971, the emphasis of policy objectives had shifted. Schools were urged to 'demonstrate how people from different ethnic groups and cultural backgrounds can live together happily and successfully, and can help to create the kind of cohesive, multicultural society on which the future of this country — and possibly the world — depends' (DES, 1971). Throughout the 1970s references to Britain as a 'multicultural society' appeared increasingly in DES publications. Authorities were told that such a conception of society had relevance to the education of all children and implications for the work of all teachers, whatever the ethnic composition of their particular schools; by the time the 'great debate' on the curriculum got underway this view had assumed a central place in DES statements about the curriculum. The 1977 Green Paper, *Education in Schools: A Consultative Document*, for example, emphasized the importance of all children being given an understanding both of the plural nature of British society and of Britain's place in an interdependent world. In a subsequently much-quoted passage the Green Paper argued that 'Our society is a multicultural, multiracial one, and the curriculum should reflect a sympathetic understanding of the different cultures and races that now make up our society ... the curriculum of our schools ... must reflect the needs of this new Britain' (DES, 1977). In 1981 the Department's important paper on *The School Curriculum* — the result of 'several years of public discussion and Government consultation with its education partners' — was categoric about the extent to which teaching in all schools should give positive recognition to the cultural diversity present in society:

> What is taught in schools, and the way it is taught, must appropriately reflect fundamental values in our society ... the work of schools has to reflect many issues with which pupils will have to come to terms as they mature, and schools and teachers are familiar with them. First, our society has become multicultural and there is now among pupils and parents a greater diversity of personal values ... (HMSO, 1981).

Policy and Practice

At the level of overall policy there has, then, been significant change. Broad 'multicultural' objectives have been laid down, and policy has become that the presence of minority ethnic groups in British society should be made a positive feature in the education of all children. By 1979 Eric Bolton, a senior HM Inspector with responsibilities in this field, was arguing that the two issues of the nature of educational provision in multiracial schools and the nature of provision for all pupils in a pluralist society were not only 'interrelated but interdependent' (Bolton, 1979). Pluralist aims have far-reaching implications for all pupils and all teachers. In the context of a broadly assimilationist approach the main need is to help minority ethnic group pupils to adapt linguistically and culturally to the existing school system. But a *pluralist* aim requires that an awareness of the diverse character of contemporary society became an integral part of many aspects of teaching — and this depends on teachers reappraising a wide range of their existing approaches.

Since the mid-1970s there has been growing recognition of what is involved for teachers. The implications are no longer predominantly seen in terms of assessing and meeting the particular needs of minority ethnic group children or as involving peripheral modifications to curriculum content, but are increasingly considered to necessitate a reappraisal of teaching strategies, forms of school organization and curriculum approaches as a whole. The DES has rightly characterized what is required as 'the re-orientation of our education system to serve a multiracial society' (HMSO, 1978), and this involves action which will permeate the whole of the education process.

But although there have been significant developments at the level of theoretical official policy, progress in implementing the new objectives has been slow. A 1979 Schools Council survey which received information from ninety-four LEAs and 525 secondary schools found that although many of those working in multiracial authorities and schools accepted the need for major curriculum development work to make their teaching relevant and appropriate for a multicultural society and that significant initiatives were taking place in some schools, work of this kind both on content and on strategies for change was at an early stage and 'substantial structural support' was necessary if it was to be developed effectively (Little and Willey, 1981). This survey also showed that DES assertions about a multicultural society having relevance to all schools had, in particular, made minimal impact. Most authorities and schools with few or no pupils from minority ethnic groups invariably reported that they thought a multicultural society was not a matter which concerned them, and that it would have low priority against more pressing calls on their energies. It was clear from the survey that developments at policy level had not been effectively carried through into classroom practice, and that major initiatives were necessary if schools in these areas were to be convinced of the relevance of a multicultural society to their teaching.

Particular Educational Needs

One aspect of DES policy has been to argue that a multicultural objective has relevance to all schools. The other major issue presented by the presence of minority ethnic group pupils was how to respond to their particular educational needs. In general, British educational policy has in practice long accepted that equality of opportunity means more and different for some if equal access to educational chances is to be a reality for all. In many ways, the concept of making provision to meet particular needs is entrenched in the education system; the idea was enshrined in the Plowden Report, the Rate Support Grant has been weighted in favour of urban areas, Educational Priority Programmes have been developed and Social Priority Schools established (Little and Robbins, 1982). As Shipman argues, 'The ROSLA programmes, Schools Council and other curriculum projects, schemes for differentially allocating central and local government funds, and for building up support services around schools, have, with accompanying secondary school reorganisation, all been influenced by the philosophy that more should go to those who face most difficulty', and indeed that 'the common element in much educational policy in the last twenty years has been positive discrimination' (Shipman, 1980). Despite this, the DES's general approach to minority ethnic groups has been to locate their particular needs firmly in the context of general policies aimed at educational disadvantage.

The main specific means by which central government has intervened directly to meet the particular needs of minority ethnic group pupils — Section 11 of the Local Government Act, 1966 — has proved to have important weaknesses. Section 11 enabled LEAs with 2 per cent or more Commonwealth immigrant pupils in their total school population to claim a 50 per cent (later raised to 75 per cent) grant towards expenditure in respect to the employment of staff. Provision is not limited to education, but in practice Section 11 has been predominantly used for claiming teachers' salaries, and an estimated 85 per cent of £50 million was allocated for this purpose in 1980/81. The Act is administered by the Home Office, and the terms and procedures have not enabled the DES to adopt the positive leadership necessary to encourage LEAs to do what they might otherwise not have done. LEAs are not required to ensure that Section 11 appointments relate to any general appraisal of the need for special provision in their areas, or that their use is part of any concerted strategy. Authorities are under no obligation to distinguish staff paid for in this way from other staff, and these appointments are often subsumed within overall staffing levels. There is no scrutiny beyond a purely financial audit and the DES does not monitor how the grant is used. The initiative for making a claim rests with the local authority and take-up has been very uneven. As the Parliamentary Home Affairs Committee, which reviewed the working of Section 11 in 1981, commented, 'there is no single aspect of Section 11 payments which has escaped criticism' (HMSO, 1981). Many LEAs in practice welcome the considerable freedom of action which the operation of Section 11 has allowed them, but it remains a fact that many teachers funded under the major scheme designed to meet minority ethnic groups' particular needs simply merge into the general staffing of schools and are not even identifiable as meeting any specific need. As the Home Affairs Committee commented, 'lowering the teacher-pupil ratio must be beneficial for all pupils, but Section 11 should not have become a mechanism for this simple end' (*op. cit.*).

In general, DES policy has been to view the particular needs of minority ethnic groups in the context of overall policies to alleviate deprivation and disadvantage. In 1973 the Parliamentary Select Committee on Race Relations and Immigration, after a major survey of educational provision, argued that more innovative and precisely targeted policies were necessary. The Committee recommended that a specialist advisory unit be set up to assess minority ethnic groups' particular educational needs, and that a central fund should be established to provide resources to meet them (HMSO, 1973). But the DES rejected the proposal for a special fund; and, in opting for a general 'Educational Disadvantage Unit' within the Department and an external 'Centre of Information and Advice on Educational Disadvantage' (subsequently to be disbanded in 1979 as part of government expenditure cuts), firmly placed the needs of minority ethnic groups within the context of overall responses to disadvantage. The rationale was that 'where immigrants and their descendants live in the older urban industrial areas, the majority of their children are likely to share with the indigenous children of these areas the educational disadvantages associated with an impoverished environment.... The pattern of special help must thus provide for all those suffering educational disadvantage' (DES, 1974). When the Select Committee again pressed for a special fund, in 1977, they were again turned down, on the grounds that 'as the most fundamental needs of ethnic minorities are essentially the same as those of the population as a whole, it is through the general expenditure programme of central and local government that these needs should be met' (HMSO, 1978). But the point at issue in the Select Committee's recommendations — and it was also made in many other reports and research surveys — was that minority ethnic groups, in addition to the extent to which some of them might share aspects of disadvantage with other groups in society, had particular needs which required particular provision.

In replying to the Select Committee's *Report on the West Indian*

Community in 1978, the DES was prepared to acknowledge that, 'as well . . . as sharing in the general problems of urban deprivation and unemployment, the West Indian Community and other ethnic minorities have certain special problems which we call by the shorthand term "racial disadvantage"' (DES, 1978). The Department accepted a recommendation to set up a Committee of Inquiry which was asked to give 'early and particular attention' to the needs of West Indians. In 1981 this Committee, the Rampton (later Swann) Committee, produced an interim Report which urged the need for a comprehensive 'programme of action' directed specifically at the needs of West Indians (DES, 1981). Running throughout the Committee's recommendations — on pre-school provision, on reading and language, on the curriculum, on teaching materials, on links between school and community, on teacher education — was an emphasis on the need for more closely focused policy and provision. The Committee specifically criticized linking minority ethnic group needs with those of other disadvantaged groups in society: 'Within the DES itself we have been concerned to note that the needs of ethnic minority children are often seen only as an aspect of educational disadvantage or in some cases just as a form of handicap. This seems to reflect a general view throughout the education service that ethnic minority children are a "problem" and in some way "lacking" or "inadequate"'. There has as yet been no clear indication whether the Department's conversion to recognizing particular needs, marked by the setting up of the Rampton/Swann Committee, will carry through to implementing the Report's recommendations — although it is now over two years since the Report was published.

LEA Responses

Early response at LEA level to the presence of minority ethnic group pupils was dominated by the immediate need to teach English to those for whom it was a second language. The way in which this could best be done was regarded as very much a matter for local authority discretion. The DES intermittently offered general advice. *English for Immigrants* (DES, 1963), for example, emphasized the need for 'a carefully planned, intensive course making full use of modern methods of language teaching', and argued that at both junior and secondary level 'special classes should be staffed by teachers with some knowledge of modern methods of teaching English as a second language.' But in practice few specialist English as a second language (E2L) teachers existed, there were no established in-service courses to train them and limited relevant materials for them to use. These circumstances, together with the natural working of Britain's decentralized education system, led to wide variations in the scale and nature of the provision made by LEAs. When Townsend surveyed the position for the NFER in 1971, he found that it was 'impossible to study immigrant education in detail without forming the impression that some local authorities place a much higher priority on arrangements for schools with immigrant pupils than do others' (Townsend, 1971).

But there were, during the 1960s and early 1970s, certain significant overall characteristics of LEA provision. Authorities were in practice almost exclusively preoccupied with meeting basic E2L needs, and providing for these determined both the organizational and conceptual response to minority groups. The main issue presented by immigration was seen as the need to enable children who did not speak English to take their place in normal classes. This was a matter for specialist language teachers, often working in centres physically separated from schools, and regarded by most as having few implications for mainstream teachers. As Rosen and Burgess describe early attitudes:

> Those children who could not speak English or who were still beyond doubt in the early stages of learning it were somebody else's business. The English as a second language teachers would give them sufficient mastery of English to equip them to enter the English as a mother tongue classroom. Once there they would be essentially no different from other pupils in the classroom. Business as usual (Rosen and Burgess, 1981).

But pluralist objectives have direct relevance to all teachers, and by the second half of the 1970s there were significant changes in LEA policies. At one level, many authorities set up specialist curriculum development and resource teams in addition to their E2L services. Examples are Coventry which established a 'Minority Groups Support Service', and Haringey which, in 1978, set up a 'Multicultural Support Group'. The Haringey team circulated a statement of aims and objectives to all teachers in the authority, and initiated a programme of visits to all schools to discuss with teachers the proposition that 'The multicultural curriculum is one which is appropriate to the education of all pupils, whatever their background, by reference to a diversity of cultures.' The Support Group undertakes a wide range of development projects which have originated from requests made by schools, heads, subject departments and individual teachers (Haringey, 1981).

But there has also been recognition that implementation of multicultural objectives has more pervasive implications for LEA provision. As Bev Woodroffe, the ILEA's Senior Inspector for multi-ethnic education has emphasized, 'the development of policy into practice has to be a priority in *all* branches and parts of an LEA' (Woodroffe, 1982). ILEA has consequently placed provision of specialist curriculum development resources firmly in the context of an overall approach which emphasizes that 'the issues of a multicultural society must be seen by London teachers as central to providing good education for all children.' This view is shared by many of the specialist Advisers for Multicultural Education appointed by LEAs during the 1970s. These Advisers have increasingly turned their attention to influencing their authorities' overall provision; many now emphasize that in addition to being responsible for seeing that the LEA meets the particular needs of minority ethnic group pupils, they are concerned with working with their colleagues in the Advisory service and through them having an effect on mainstream provision. A growing number of LEAs are incorporating commitment to multicultural and pluralist objectives into their formal policy aims.

Approaches in Schools

During the early 1970s much of the innovative work carried out in multiracial schools was undertaken by individual teachers. Initial response often concentrated on a 'Black Studies' approach — the development of specialist additions to the established curriculum, such as topics and lessons on West Indian history or Indian music. Responding to minority ethnic groups was seen as a matter of special provision at the periphery of normal school activity. At secondary stage, for example, committed staff often developed CSE Mode 3 courses. But many headteachers and heads of department in multiracial schools now consider that more concerted action affecting the school as a whole and involving all staff is needed. A 1979 Schools Council survey of 225 secondary schools in multiracial areas found that in 68 per cent (and in 98 per cent of those with 30 per cent or more pupils from minority ethnic groups) the implications of pluralist objectives had been discussed at meetings of senior staff or all staff. Typical comments from teachers were 'at one level this is a matter for the ethos of the whole school', 'an "across the curriculum" approach involving all staff is desirable', 'no one area of the curriculum can be singled out as being particularly important — rather the permeation of topics and issues throughout the curriculum' (Little and Willey, 1981). Heads and heads of departments in these schools are under no illusions about the implications of this sort of analysis of what is required; it is seen as involving a comprehensive review of existing practice in which staff should be as widely involved as possible.

Increasingly, 'whole school' approaches are being adopted to considering the implications of multicultural objectives for classroom practice. A common initial starting point is to set up a working party to consider priorities relevant to a school's particular situation. Such working parties then act as a focus for initiating and sustaining wider discussion among staff. Fifty-eight per cent of schools with a concentration of minority ethnic group pupils reported to the Schools Council survey that they had established such working parties. In one school where a working party spent two years producing a detailed report examining 'the whole work and ethos of the school in the light of its multicultural nature', the background was the working party's view that 'there is an overriding need to pursue positive policies of cultural awareness across the whole of school life. Multicultural education will not just happen, rather prejudice and institutionalised discrimination will dominate' (Birley High School, 1980).

Another example is a comprehensive school where the heads of department meeting set up a working party which produced a series of questions which they considered 'every teacher in the school should ask him/herself . . . and then compare notes within a department.' The questions included such things as consideration of underlying bias and stereotyping in attitudes and teaching approaches, examination of the appropriateness of textbooks and materials to a multicultural society, and analysis of the performance of minority ethnic group pupils as individuals and as a group. Each department in the school was then asked to consider 'the implications for their department of operating in a multicultural school . . . [and to] see how well or ill-equipped they are for this, and what developments would be helpful' (Wood Green School, 1979). This sort of procedure can create a framework in which whole-school approaches can be developed which provide teachers with the opportunity jointly of contributing to working out an overall school policy. In an increasing number of schools such initiatives are resulting in explicit recognition of pluralist objectives being incorporated into the formal aims of the school.

In practice, detailed consideration within schools of the application of pluralist objectives is a complex process. This is both because the widely varying attitudes in society towards responding to ethnic and cultural diversity are reflected among teachers, and because educational questions arise to which the rhetoric of official policy pronouncements provides no readily applicable answers. Difficult decisions have to be made, for example, about the degree and nature of diversity which the school should encourage and endorse, and the relationship of this to the need to provide pupils with the knowledge and understanding which they require to operate in the world outside school. It is at classroom level that the divergence between pluralist ideals and the realities of contemporary society is being confronted.

As Alan James argues, 'teachers have to consider how "multiculturalism" can be made a rational educational ideology in a society whose institutions are not necessarily geared to tolerant pluralism' (James, 1979). Teachers are faced by the need both to educate children in positive attitudes towards cultural diversity and to teach them about how and why the society in which they live actually functions. In constructing an educationally valuable curriculum which is relevant to a multicultural society, teachers also have to accept the challenge of and opportunity for appraisal and evaluation which diverse cultures offer. As Paul Zec has warned, a sentimental 'valuing' of all aspects of a culture which are different from a teacher's own is essentially as anti-educational as ethnocentrism (Zec, 1980). Educational judgements have to be made which often involve schools in protracted debate. As the head of one London comprehensive, where current thinking is that 'our multicultural world should be much more firmly embedded in the daily classroom experience of students', describes the scale of what is involved:

> ... real and positive developments in a school, involving staff at all levels with democratic debate and decision-making, is a slow, difficult and sometimes painful process. As well as curriculum review, our systems of organisation need examination. Having stated our aims and begun the business of analysing our practice we need to invent, criticise and modify as we go along (Wilson, 1983).

Only when this process of debate and analysis is entered into widely by teachers can pluralist aims be transmuted from the vague ideals of official pronouncement into actual classroom practice.

Richard Willey

Combatting Racism

Although multicultural objectives have gained a central place at national policy level, such aims are generally enunciated without specific reference to current black-white relations in society. In 1981, when the DES commended six broad educational aims as 'a checklist against which Local Authorities and schools can test their curricular policies and their application to individual schools', two of the six related directly to a culturally diverse society: '(iv) to instill respect for religious and moral values, and tolerance of other races, religions and ways of life; (v) to help pupils to understand the world in which they live, and the interdependence of individuals, groups and nations' (DES, 1981). In practice, teaching about tolerance and about the relations between groups in society must address directly the realities of contemporary race relations. The context in which teachers are being asked to develop pluralist objectives is one in which the operation of racial prejudice and discrimination is a well-documented reality (Smith, 1977), and in which it has been considered necessary to introduce progressively strengthened anti-discrimination legislation — the Race Relations Acts of 1965, 1968 and 1976.

Experience in multiracial schools shows that if teachers are to develop objectives of equality and pluralism, the thread of responding to the fact of discrimination has to run through many aspects of school life. Response to the effects of prejudice has to be made explicit in the curriculum, in teaching materials, in forms of school organization, in self-examination by teachers of their own attitudes, in dealing with overt racialist behaviour, in formal school policies. Attention in developing responses to cultural diversity is increasingly turning to the need to confront the central fact of racism; a discussion paper circulated by Berkshire LEA, for example, argues, 'The principal emphasis in the 1980s, it is suggested, should be on equality. This will certainly involve attention to racism, and to measures to unlearn and dismantle racism' (Berkshire LEA, 1982). Combatting racial discrimination is being seen as an integral part of developing multicultural objectives. In 1982 the then head of the ILEA told teachers that each school should have a

> clear view, agreed within itself, on how it is to deal with discriminatory practices wherever they may show themselves. The obligation is plain. The education service must concern itself with everyone in this City, every child and every parent of every child must know where we stand. Whatever its

source, wherever it lies, however it manifests itself, the education service is flatly opposed to racial discrimination (ILEA, 1982).

Schools adopting this sort of approach consider that such policies are integral to providing equality in a multicultural society. The point is made strongly in a statement on racist behaviour included in the handbook of a London comprehensive:

> In the staff handbook the first aim of Quintin Kynaston school is to demonstrate that we regard all students as being of equal value. Racism is diametrically opposed to this aim and must therefore be positively resisted by the school. It is important that everybody associated with Quintin Kynaston see the school's policy on racism as a natural part of the responsibilities of a comprehensive school (ILEA, 1982).

Conclusion

Significant developments have taken place in the educational response to cultural diversity. There is now an overall policy commitment to multicultural aims. In some LEAs and schools the far-reaching and complex implications of implementing such objectives are being worked out. Pervasive 'whole school' approaches are being adopted. But there has been limited concerted action to secure systematic change in all schools; in particular, little has been done to give children in schools with few or no minority ethnic group pupils a positive awareness of cultural diversity. Structural support for teachers is necessary to enable them to narrow the gap between theoretical policy and much classroom practice.

References

BERKSHIRE LEA (1982) *Education for Equality*, Advisory Committee for Multicultural Education, Department of Education, Berkshire.

BIRLEY HIGH SCHOOL (1980) *Multi-cultural Education in the 1980s: The Report of a Working Party of Teachers at Birley High School*, Manchester, City of Manchester Education Committee.

BOLTON, E. (1979) 'Education in a multi-racial society', *Trends in Education*, 4.

DES (1963) *English for Immigrants*, Pamphlet No. 43, London, HMSO.

DES (1965) *The Employment and Distribution of Teachers*, Circular 1/65 London.

DES (1971) *The Education of Immigrants*, Survey 13, London, HMSO.

DES (1974) *Educational Disadvantage and the Educational Needs of Immigrants*, London, HMSO.

DES (1977) *Education in Schools: A Consultative Document*, Cmnd, 6869, London, HMSO.

DES (1981) *The School Curriculum*, London, HMSO.

DES (1981) *West Indian Children in Our Schools* ('Rampton Report'), Interim Report of the Committee of Inquiry into the Education of Children from Ethnic Minority Groups, Cmnd, 8273, ('Rampton Report') London, HMSO.

HARINGEY LEA (1981) *Multi-Cultural Curriculum Support Group, First Report, 1979–81*, Borough of Haringey.

HMSO (1973) *Education*, Report of the Select Committee on Race Relations and Immigration, London.

HMSO (1978) *The West Indian Community. Observations on the Report of the Select Committee on Race Relations and Immigration*, Cmnd, 7186, London.

HMSO (1981) *Racial Disadvantage*, Report of the Home Affairs Committee, Session 1980–81, London.

ILEA (1982) *Anti-Racist School Policies*, London.

JAMES, A. (1981) 'The "multi-cultural" curriculum', in JAMES, A. and JEFFCOATE, R. (Eds), *The School in the Multicultural Society*, Harper and Row.

LITTLE, A. and ROBBINS, D. (1982) *Loading the Law: A Study of Transmitted Deprivation, Ethnic Minorities and Affirmative Action*, CRE.

LITTLE, A. and WILLEY, R. (1981) *Multi-ethnic Education: The Way Forward*, Schools Council, London.

ROSE, E.J.B. *et al.* (1969) *Colour and Citizenship*, Oxford, OUP.

ROSEN, H. and BURGESS, T. (1981) *Language and Dialects of London School Children*, Ward Lock.

SHIPMAN, M. (1980) 'The limits of positive discrimination', in MARLAND, (Ed.) *Education for the Inner City*, London, Heinemann.

SMITH, D.J. (1977) *Racial Disadvantage in Britain*, Harmondsworth, Penguin.

TOWNSEND, H.E.R. (1971) *Immigrant Pupils in England: The LEA Response*, Windsor, NFER.

WILSON, A. (1983) 'The development of multi-cultural policy and practice at Walsingham School', *Multi-Ethnic Education Review*, 2, I.

WOODROFFE, B. (1982) '1977–1982: Multi-ethnic education in ILEA', *Multi-Ethnic Education Review*, I, 2.

ZEC, P. (1981) 'Multi-cultural education: What kind of relativism is possible', in JAMES, A. and JEFFCOATE, R. (Eds) *The School in the Multicultural Society*, Harper and Row.

Curriculum and Assessment

James Lynch

This paper briefly considers some of the conceptual and operational strategies and dilemmas of curriculum construction and pupil assessment in a multicultural society, in the broader context of social change.

There is no position of centrality from which to survey developments towards a curriculum for multicultural education in the United Kingdom of the early 1980s. Neither is there any overall unity of view with regard to what that term might mean, let alone what such negotiated common meaning might imply in being put into action. Even the basic nomenclature is in dispute, focusing alternately on race, ethnicity, religion, language and culture, seen now as synonymous, now as mutually exclusive and now as overlapping. Words to be descriptive of major ethnic minority groups are in some cases not yet agreed.

The Parochialism of the Debate

In such circumstances it behoves an author to make clear from the beginning that however widely and liberally he seeks to cast his net his view is likely to be something less than comprehensive and something more than partial. Moreover, these problems of incompleteness and partiality are accentuated by the peculiarly ethnocentric and parochial base around which the whole multicultural education debate has revolved in the United Kingdom. With a few notable exceptions, including the curriculum area of world studies, relatively little discussion has taken place of models of multicultural education from overseas, either in the other countries of Europe or even the English-speaking nations of North America and Australasia, let alone elsewhere. Consideration of such models might well have facilitated the evolution of a cross-cultural approach and the articulation of the 'overarching principles of rationality',[1] so essential to gaining real purchase on the fundamental issues and decisions associated with relatively new-found perceptions of British society as being multicultural.[2] But alas, in spite of a multitude of close-quarters skirmishes, much entrenched posturing and long-range polemical bombardment, the 'high ground' of multicultural education has hardly begun to be taken, and major issues have remained 'interned' and therefore unavailable for that public discourse which can give access to the generation of new norms of behaviour and criteria for the judgement of that behaviour.

Having made such a depressing disclaimer, let me hasten to say that only the purblind would claim that no progress has been made or that the momentum of the debate is not mounting; and that it would be cavalier and unjust to dismiss as insignificant the multitude of good-hearted strivings in this field to introduce new curriculum developments, particularly school-based and teacher-initiated, to expose inequity in the system and reasons for it, to fight racism and discrimination and to provide the political and legal foundations for a healthy, cultural pluralism in British society. But the fact remains that much of the curriculum debate has focused too exclusively on issues of English as a second language, on multicredal or comparative religion, on Black or Asian Studies, either additively to existing curricula, representing dominant interests, or cocooned within existing subject capsules as in the rewriting of aspects of history or geography. I do not intend to be disparaging about these innovations, some of which may yet prove to be important nodal points from which to fight problems such as racism, or even exploratory precursors of more widespread and fundamental curricular reform. I am making a different and more general point, namely, that combined with the parochialism of the debate referred to above, such initiatives have tended to set the outside parameters for that debate rather than being seen as enlivening and creative contributions to it. Then again, as the Select Committee Report of 1982 pointed out, some curriculum developments of this kind may run the danger of 'ghettoizing' the curriculum for ethnic minority children, reinforcing existing hierarchies of knowledge and postponing the achievement of consensus about more fundamental reforms demanded by a multicultural society.[3] This brief paper therefore seeks to sample and culturally locate the kinds of initiatives which have taken place, and furthermore, to indicate what seem to the author promising and sometimes pressing avenues for likely further debate and clarification.

National Developments

At the national level and in terms of political initiatives, while the much-demanded governmental policy statement confirming the multicultural nature of British society had not appeared by early 1983 and did not seem likely to appear within the near future,[4] the 1976 Race Relations Act provided an apparent benchmark against which progress and aspiration could be measured at more lowly levels in all sectors, not least in education. The confirmation by High Court Appeal, arising from the complaint of an Asian adolescent that the Sikhs constituted a racial group, seemed indication that the Act had teeth and that legal norms had been created. Then, too, many LEAs had published policy statements on multicultural education, racism and equal opportunities, sometimes including overall statements on employment,[5] and schools also had evolved similar antiracial and multicultural statements and curricula.[6]

But in spite of all this and much more besides, the continuing reticence of government[7] and the majority of local authorities[8] to issue policy statements seemed by late 1983 to be holding back the growth of those norms of morality and custom which are equally as fundamental as are legal norms to social cohesion. For paradox though it may seem, one of the commonalities of a multicultural society is its espousal of difference in practice, in morality and in custom as in law, for law is purposive — rational and manipulative, and therefore may not be productive of the personality-enhancing norms that will build a community and education for that community which is intrinsically multicultural. In this respect the work of the Commission for Racial Equality and the local Community Relations Councils in disseminating information, building good relationships, providing advice and counsel, and gently persuading the recalcitrant does not make the headlines as a rule but is a vital part of such community building. To this has to be added the work of countless organizations and associations, from the Schools Council[9] and the National Association for Multiracial Education to cultural, professional and occupational groups such as the National Union of Teachers, which have unequivocally endorsed the multiculturalism of British society and its implications for education, and whose members are at the very fulcrum of norm-building interaction with the next generation and the present in the form of children, parents and the wider community.[10] Then, too, regional groups have grown up, such as ALTARF (All London Teachers against Racism Front) and AFFOR (All Faiths for One Race), and have often had influence far beyond their original location. New resource centres have been established, such as ACER (the Afro-Caribbean European Resource Project); a new centre has been set up at Bulmershe College of Higher Education as a kind of 'exchange and mart' for information about multicultural education resources; and new journals have been established, such as *Multicultural Education Abstracts*, and more recently 'for practitioners in school and community', *Multicultural Teaching*. Thus there is a very real benchmark against which modest progress and substantial achievement may be tallied.

The Effect on the Curriculum and Examinations

But teachers seek their effect through a mechanism that we call a curriculum — a planned programme for knowledge and value transmission to the young, which is validated and legitimated by a further sub- (but in fact controlling) system that we call examinations. The real litmus test of the advance of norms of multicultural education might therefore logically be the extent of manifested response of the fundamental ethic and generative norms of multiculturalism in that cultural fulcrum and its control mechanism.

If, as Jeffcoate has argued,[11] the fundamental ethic of a multicultural society is respect for persons, then this must imply, through the principle of mutuality, that there can be no discrimination against individuals or groups on the basis of their racial or broader cultural characteristics, provided that the latter are congruent with the basic ethic itself. This in turn must mean that all cultural groups which themselves espouse the basic ethic must have equality of access to aspects of society's structures and institutions such as the law and education, and to economic rewards and resources. In education, this must involve as a fundamental the active pursuit of equality of educational opportunity, which means that in implementing multicultural education we are faced with a 'philosophy' at least equal in magnitude to comprehensive education in its implications for school structure, knowledge and assessment. Here the evidence for such equality is depressing, to say the least. Concern about the educational performance of ethnic minority children (considered in detail by Dr Peter Figueroa in this volume, pp. 117–141) can be traced back to the early 1960s, but tended to be explained by their recency of arrival. Work from the 1970s indicated increasingly, however, that the problem was not transient. Not only were 'immigrant' children underachieving, but pupils from ethnic minority groups who had been born in Britain and fully educated here were still under-functioning in comparison with other majority pupils.[12] Ethnic minority children were frequently found in the bottom streams,[13] and certain ethnic minority group children were being labelled educationally subnormal to a frighteningly unconvincing degree.[14] The doctrine of recency of arrival as an explanation of unequal performance, as a 'transient' phenomenon, was thus thrown into disarray. More recently, of thirty-three studies summarized by Tomlinson of the educational achievement of children of West Indian origins, twenty-six showed them to score lower than whites or to be overrepresented in ESN schools or underrepresented in high streams of normal schools.[15] Similarly, Taylor's review of the research on the education of West Indian pupils showed a strong trend towards underachievement on their part against the main conventional indicators of academic performance.[16]

Moreover, when broader strategies have been adopted in the research to include developmental status, school achievements and post-secondary outcomes, it was discovered that minority children, and especially those of West Indian origin, lagged behind non-minority children from the pre-school years to late adolescence, and have thus been handicapped in both further education and employment.[17] When research has included ethnically mixed samples of students matched for social class, the performance of West Indian pupils in public examinations has been reported to be lower than for all other groups,[18] although the picture is more complex than this simple statement would imply when it comes to staying on in the sixth form and access to further and higher education. This latter and some other studies have indicated important distinctions, not just between the performance of minority and non-minority children, but also between groups such as West Indian children and Asian children, internally within minority children as a whole, and between white and Asian pupils. Thus, while it would be simplistic in the extreme to imagine a plain hierarchical relationship between race, ethnicity and achievement some of the major trends are discernible with a degree of clarity.[19] Many other studies could also be quoted and in some cases, no doubt, there are flaws and mistakes in the methodology and therefore limitations on the interpretations which can be made and the inferences which can be drawn. One thing, however, is clear, namely that, however defined or attempted, the United Kingdom is a very long way from achieving equality of educational opportunity for large numbers of ethnic minority pupils in our society, with both academic qualification and job consequences; and that, amid much other neglect, there are some quite fundamental issues concerning the contribution of the education system in general and of curriculum and assessment in particular to these inequalities that have not yet been faced.

It follows that, purely in terms of scale, tinkering with portions of the curriculum or adding a 'folksy' flavouring to existing curricula is unlikely to effect real change, and thus achieve greater equality of educational opportunity for those presently marginalized from such access. It also follows that unless the social and cultural control mechanisms can be relaxed and reformed in step with reforms in the content and process of education, there can be much curriculum innovation but little fundamental change affording such greater equality of educational opportunity and thus access to occupational and social mobility. For, without arguing that only extrinsic rewards are provided by education, unless both content and control are changed, only that knowledge which is 'validated' will by and large be societally available for 'trading' to achieve access to resources.[20] However gently and patronizingly, other knowledge will be bracketted 'differently'. Thus any fundamental curriculum change which is to be more than a mere legitimating mechanism has to be accompanied *pari passu* by examination reform, including the calibration of those examinations in higher education with the world of work more specifically and with society in general. (One alternative to this position is to engage in active social valuing of others' cultures, but to stop short of economically consequential valuing, hoping that this approach may reduce conflict, suggest equality and legitimate the economic *status quo*, rather than liberate pupils from autocratic culture-bound economic discrimination, and therefore disadvantage: an ethical position of dubious morality and inimical to the basic principles of a multicultural society.)

The Implications of Commitment to Multicultural Education

Commitment to an education appropriate to the multicultural nature of our society — multicultural education for short — compels us to a long agenda of changes, focused on the achievement of greater equality of educational opportunity. It confronts us not just with one pluralist dilemma, but with a whole series for the resolution of which we need to master new expertise, skills and knowledge,[21] and above all to marshall a new political will. We require, for instance, some commonly accepted, if transitional, agreement about the bounds of our multiculturalism. There is the question of whether it is a worldwide one, or one bounded by the parameters of our nation state, albeit drawing on traditions such as the rule of law which have achieved more universal recognition. If both, then the question follows, in what measure and according to what criteria? Nor is it possible, given our human condition as products of a given cultural milieu, to hope to entirely escape by dint of cross-culturally valid rationality to arrive at a 'culture-free' solution.

If 'the enculturation imperative — the need to have enough of a common culture passed on to each generation of children', as Bullivant describes it,[22] is seen as a valid social imperative, then we need to clarify who decides on that commonality and through what process. Furthermore, what do such decisions imply in terms of 'alternatives' selected from the total multicultural capital available to our society? How are decisions arrived at regarding inclusion — or exclusion — from that valued knowledge that we call a curriculum? I have argued elsewhere that such questions imply agreement on a core curriculum for our schools,[23] a complex issue already hotly debated, and a term subject to many interpretations and much misinterpretation. One course open to us, therefore, is to strive by discourse for the achievement of logically consistent decisions representing the nearest to consensus which can be achieved, subject to continuing reappraisal and evaluation.

An Initial Curriculum Dilemma

But how far is such a discourse logically possible in modern society? By what criteria could it be judged to be balanced, i.e. fair, and is it compatible with the statutory responsibilities? Could it involve, for instance, curriculum prescription by a Secretary of State — at least as far as the core is concerned — with all the dangers which such prescriptions might imply: a course of action congruent with the traditions of some other European countries, but until recently seen as alien to British educational traditions. Moreover, if this were the case, would this imply that all pupils at all schools would be exposed to this core of 'basic and essential learnings required of all pupils in all schools'; and 'embodying multicultural experiences and ideals',[24] including public and private, county and voluntary schools, and would this mean a renegotiation and rewriting of the 1944 Settlement? The contradictions here are those, firstly, of educational provision which will be common when differentiation may be necessary to achieve greater equality,[25] or differentiated provision to take account of unequal starting points which may therefore be automatically uneven. (Currently, we have a public policy of differentiation legitimated by a myth of universalism.) Secondly, there is the apparent but not insuperable contradiction of the need for some kind of prescription, however broad the parameters, if the core is to be common, contrasted with the need for adaptive and creative curricularizing on the part of schools to be fostered if they are not to become divorced from their communities, esoteric in their selection of knowledge and mere routinized bureaucratized 'instruction (and assessment) factories'.

The Assessment Dimension

But let us suppose for a moment that we have 'cleared the decks', achieved provisional consensus about the commonalities of our multicultural society, and through that the basic and essential learnings which are needed by *all* pupils to provide for the social imperative referred to above of providing social continuity but not merely maintenance. How do we monitor the achievement of that core; or, put another way, the progress of all pupils through these core learning experiences in a way which does not discriminate on the basis of culture, i.e. race, religion, ethnicity etc., but leads to comparable schooling and outcomes? Here the Schools Council has taken one or two modest initiatives with far-reaching implications. In addition to requesting all its subject committees to bear the multicultural dimension in mind in considering national criteria for the new 16+ examinations, established in 1981, it has initiated a review of examination provision in eleven subject areas to assess how far current provision meets or could be developed to meet the needs of a multicultural society.[26] The aims of that project are significant for they envisage the development of:

> — examinations within the major subject areas that draw from a wider range of cultures than hitherto, and that are as a result less culturally biased and more empathetic to the multicultural nature of our society;
> — examinations with particular cultural emphases that both better serve the current needs of ethnic minority candidates, and that also are accessible to all pupils, irrespective of their cultural backgrounds.[27]

In view of the subsequent furore which emerged over the non-publication of the Geography Report by the Council,[28] it will be apparent that this area is fraught with complexity and explosive dynamism, but it is also creatively generative of potential for fundamental reform. For if, as proposed, a common examination system is introduced and, bearing in mind the depressing conclusions of one expert on examinations that in general 'compatibility is a myth',[29] then the way is cleared for the first time for progress towards greater equality of performance across both social class and ethnic lines in a way which would not have been thought possible a few years ago. In this sense, the gingerly drawn terms of reference of the Schools Council Assessment in a Multicultural Society Project may well prove to have been both timely and politically and sensitively enough forged to achieve 'social space' for incipient movement towards reform.

This is not to ignore the continued requirement of the educational system in our society to perform a selection function by means of examinations, nor is it to be starry-eyed about the control function of those examinations *vis-à-vis* the curriculum. On the other hand, it is to see in this latter linkage opportunities for influencing curriculum, from the power end for a change, to be more appropriate to our multicultural society and its need for greater equality of educational opportunity. Such an opening has not presented itself previously, and it is afforded even greater significance by the requirement of the 1980 Education Act which lays upon schools an obligation to publish their public examination results each year. Through this medium we may yet have a means of assessing the efficiency and even-handedness of education at system, institution and teacher level which we did not previously possess.

Caution is needed, of course, for no educational outcome can be restricted to a tramline of intended objectives. Nor is there any scope for the simplistic determinism which argues that certification will always work to the detriment of all but dominant social and ethnic groups — and ever more'shall be so. If that were so, we might as well sit back and do nothing but criticize a system which we know we cannot change. For me, such determinism is a counsel of despair, not only for education but also for the ethnic and social minority groups themselves. Indeed, there are alternative and rather more optimistic scenarios which are available to us, and which, while addressing that social continuity without which society would fragment into anarchy, will at the same time allow for supporting and fostering that human creativity and diversity which is a central characteristic of multicultural Britain in the 1980s. What, I would argue, we need is a more rigorous and persistent pursuit of a whole shopping list of reforms in curriculum and assessment which accept that we shall not enter the Valhalla of perfect equality until we reach the great leveller itself; but that, in the meantime, we can strive toward and succeed in improving education for a multicultural society, making it more fair, more just, more representative of our multiculture, less repressive, exclusive and socially and racially discriminating and, above all, a more effective means of achieving equality of educational opportunity.

Achieving the Goal of Greater Equality of Educational Opportunity

So what should we be aiming to do for the 1980s, to achieve both curricula and examinations which are appropriate for our changing multicultural society? How, the reader may ask, do you propose to achieve this goal? What at least in outline is your shopping list? For a start, the basic dilemma of a pluralist society which espouses democracy and freedom has to be tackled more explicitly, logically and urgently. Educationists have to stop being precious about the difficulties, and must suggest tentative working decisions about, as Craft puts it, '... at what point the acculturation necessary for full participation in society becomes a repressive assimilation; and at what point the celebration of diversity ceases to enrich and becomes potentially divisive.'[30] For as he argues, and I agree, the two are interdependent and mutually enriching if only we can come to terms with the creative tension which they inevitably imply in an imperfect but still democratic society.

A further challenge is to create the parameters within which both curriculum and examinations can grow and develop organically towards the objective of greater equality. At national level, for instance, the legal baseline has to be strengthened to dismantle existing discrimination based on racial or cultural characteristics, and current loopholes in the 1976 Act must be closed. Government must make it unequivocally clear that it recognizes our society as a multiracial and multicultural one and is committed to the pursuit of policies of equal opportunity for all legitimate cultural groups. As an employer itself, and for all 'departments' which it financially supports and/or for which it exercises ultimate executive responsibility, it should make it clear that it and they are 'equal opportunity employers'.[31] This must be a condition of continued financial support. After due consultation, a national policy statement by government on this issue should be prepared and published as a basis for each department of state to issue an analagous and interlocking statement for its own respective area of responsibility.

Getting Discourse Moving

More specifically in the field of education, a major debate is needed, based on such a national policy statement which makes manifest the Commitment of the Department of Education and Science to equality of opportunity, and to the twin fundamental values of multicultural education — namely, respect for persons, and cultural diversity conjoined in creative tension with dynamic social continuity. More general and overall guiding principles will need to be set for a common core curriculum and examinations permeated by the values of multiculturalism.[32] The Department has a responsibility to create the conditions where individual communities can implement multicultural education according to their local perceptions and needs. Each local education authority must, therefore, be encouraged to engage in creative discourse with its communities and to issue its own policy statement; and to set in motion the necessary debate about the commitment and values of the multicultural school and the overall shape of its curriculum and methods of assessment.

The in-service education of teachers for this task should be designated a national priority, perhaps building on the experience and model of the recent educational management initiative with both national and regional centres. A substantial and as yet largely neglected programme of in-service education is necessary to enable the schools to undertake this creative engagement with their own communities. Each school will need to undertake a critical social and cultural analysis of its own community and clientele before reforming its curriculum, organization, style of management, examinations and school-community relationships. Each teacher will need to examine his own teaching against collegially-generated criteria which will themselves be subject to continuing critical reappraisal.

Insofar as the curriculum itself is concerned, it must be rigorously reappraised for its cultural openness, fairness and representativeness. Materials and aids will need to be monitored for their race, sex and cultural bias and, as necessary, discarded or reformed. We must stop pretending that mother tongue teaching is an insuperable problem, and make available to each child whose parents request it, either by direct means or by vicarious ones (such as the maximization of community teaching resources, distance learning, flexistudy) the opportunity to nurture the precious cultural gift of their mother tongue. Each school must confront racism, social stereotyping and cultural bias in its content and process, and both learning experiences and substantive areas must be reformed accordingly.

Scrutiny and Reform of Examinations

As I have argued earlier, examinations are amongst the most significant control mechanisms which determine the selection of culture which is to be 'validated'. It is one of the paradoxes of educational development that at the very time when we appear on the point of achieving a common examination system which will attenuate, but not totally overcome, problems of comparability, and when we have a unified body to look at the close interrelationship of curriculum and examinations (and incidentally begin to call the latter to a multicultural accountability), government has decided to separate the two areas as the responsibilities of *two* separate national committees. But no matter, we must learn to live with that problem for the immediate future, and with renewed determination make more sure:

1 that the content, procedures and overall results of our examinations are continually monitored for any racial, social and cultural bias and corrected accordingly;
2 that the wider community has more open access to information and influence about curriculum and examinations than is the case at the moment;
3 that there is correspondingly greater accountability and opportunity for challenge of both by communities and individuals;
4 that syllabuses reflect the diversity of culture, and include a range of values and descriptions of ways of life, including those of different ethnic and racial groups, and a broader selection of subject matter;
5 that examination questions are framed in as 'culture-fair' a way as possible;
6 that multiple indicators are used to profile the diverse achievements of pupils;
7 that evaluation strategies replace narrow examination approaches.

Perhaps, too, as James Banks suggests for the United States, we need to look again at our concept of equity, and define it more in terms of educational outputs than mythically equal opportunities,[33] a view which is strengthened by Troyna's exposition of the complex and indirect relationship between educational achievement and success in the labour market.[34] If multicultural education is not to become, as he argues it is, a mere strategy of containment, its advocates have to demonstrate more convincingly its efficacy in helping to achieve greater social and educational equality, albeit bearing in mind the inevitably limited role which schools can play in broader social reform. Above all, we must keep achievement in perspective in the multicultural curriculum, and make certain that it does not become a means of 'turning off' a majority of the young people, but rather, the means of keeping the individual, community and society open to and capable of further life-long learning, not least from each other, in pursuit of still greater cultural diversity, educational equality and economic equity, achieved from the safe haven of our human and social unity.[35]

Notes

1 A discussion of this issue has emerged more recently, and has opened up the issue of the criteria for recognition of that which is worthwhile in particular cultures. See ZEC, P. (1980) 'Multicultural Education. What kind of relativism is possible?', *Journal of Philosophy of Education*, 14, pp. 77–86; WALKLING, P. (1980) 'The idea of a multicultural curriculum', *Journal of Philosophy of Education*, 14, pp. 87–95; PHILIPS-BELL, M. (1981) 'Multicultural education: A critique of Walking and Zec', *Journal of Philosophy of Education*, 15, pp. 97–105.

2 See, however, a forthcoming publication which seeks to inject a comparative dimension into the debate: CORNER, T. (Ed.) (1983 forthcoming) *Education in Multicultural Societies*, London, Croom Helm, (proceedings of the British Comparative Education Society Series); and an earlier article by WATSON, K. (1979) 'Educational policies in multicultural societies', *Comparative Education*, 15, March, pp. 17–31.

3 House of Commons, Home Affairs Committee, Session 1980–81 (1981) *Fifth Report: Racial Disadvantage*, London, HMSO, Vol. 1, p. LXVI.

4 Although, of course, reference had been made to the 'issue' of special needs in Department of Education and Science and Welsh Office (1980), *Framework for the School Curriculum*, HMSO, and to the need for work in schools to reflect the fact that society had become multicultural in Department of Education and Science and Welsh

Office (1981) *The School Curriculum*, London, HMSO, pp. 6 and 10, para 21 and 36.

5   See, for example, City of Bradford Metropolitan Council (n.d.) *Race Relations and the Council*, Bradford (approved November 1981 and reaffirmed July 1982); also 'Education for a multicultural society: Provision for pupils of ethnic minority communities', Bradford Local Authority Memorandum, 1982, cyclo.

7   This is not to ignore the statements and proposals which have been made, a brief review of which has been made by Craft, insofar as they pertain to teacher education, and myself, insofar as they enlighten the curriculum issue. See CRAFT, M. (1980) 'Recognition of need', in CRAFT, M. (Ed.), *Teaching in a Multicultural Society: The Task for Teacher Education*, Lewes, Falmer Press; and LYNCH, J. (1983) *The Multicultural Curriculum*, London, Batsford, especially Chapter 3.

8   Of course, all generalizations are invidious and one could equally well quote the policy statement of the London Borough of Brent which is path-breaking in its recognition of the intertwining of the implementation of multicultural education with curriculum theory if a 'normal' approach is to be adopted. See London Borough of Brent, Education Committee 22 March 1982, 'Report No. 44/82 of the Director of Education', including appendices.

9   For an overview of the Council's work in this field, see The Schools Council, (1982) *Multicultural Education*, London, March.

10 See in particular their early statements on multiculturalism and racial stereotyping: National Union of Teachers (1978) *All Our Children*, London, NUT, January, and (1979) *In Black and White*, London, NUT, December.

11 JEFFCOATE, R. (1976) 'Curriculum planning in multiracial education', *Educational Research*, June, pp. 192–200, and (1979) *Positive Image: Towards a Multicultural Curriculum*, London, Chameleon Books.

12 Community Relations Commission (1974) *The Educational Needs of Children from Minority Groups*, London, CRC.

13 TOWNSEND, H.E.R. and BRITTAN, E. (1972) *Organisation in Multicultural Schools*, Slough, NFER.

14 For instance, COARD, B.L. (1971) *How the West Indian Child Is Made Educationally Sub-Normal in the British School System*, London, Beacon.

15 TOMLINSON, S. (1980) 'The educational performance of ethnic minority children', *New Community*, 8, 3, Winter, pp. 213–34.

16 TAYLOR, M. (1981) *Caught Between: A Review of Research into the Education of Pupils of West Indian Origin*, Windsor, NFER-Nelson.

17 SCARR, S. *et al.* (1983) 'Developmental status and school achievements of minority and non-minority children from birth to 18 years in a British midlands town', *British Journal of Developmental Psychology*, 1, pp. 31–48.

18 CRAFT, M. and CRAFT, A.Z. (1983) 'The participation of ethnic minority pupils in further and higher education', *Educational Research*, 25, 1, pp. 10–19.

19 See, for example, Black People's Progressive Association and Redbridge

Community Relations Council (1978) *Cause for Concern: West Indian Pupils in Redbridge* Ilford, BPPA and RCRC.

20 Lashley tellingly notes that there has been very little development in examinations in response to the needs of a multicultural society and adds that, where it has taken place, it has occurred mainly in the CSE, in areas and schools with high ethnic minority concentration and in subject areas such as religious education. See LASHLEY, H. (1979) 'Examinations and the multicultural society', *Secondary Education Journal*, 9, 2, pp. 9–11. More explicitly the CRE journal stated:

No one concerned with multicultural education can afford to stay quiet about examinations. If we do so, we shall continue to limit the scope for curriculum change mainly to non-examination subjects and to lower levels of school performance, where most of the changes have been concentrated so far. (Commission for Racial Equality, 1979, *Education Journal*, 1, 3, p. 1.)

21 John Eggleston has recently commented on the naivety with which this problem has been approached in teacher education. See EGGLESTON, J. (1983) 'Ethnic naivety', *The Times Educational Supplement*, 11 March, p. 19.

22 BULLIVANT, B. (1981) *The Pluralist Dilemma in Education*, Sydney, George Allen and Unwin, p. 14.

23 LYNCH, J. (1982) 'Multicultural education and the core curriculum', *Curriculum*, 3, 1, pp. 28–34.

24 I am indebted to Malcolm Skilbeck's work for this formulation and, in particular, to his efforts to show the interdependence possible between core curriculum and school-based development. See SKILBECK, M. (1980) 'Core curriculum: An essay in cultural reconstruction', *Discourse*, 1, 1; and (1981) 'Curriculum issues in Australia, 1970–1990: Contexts, policies and practices', *Compare*, 2, 1, pp. 59–76.

25 This is one of the conclusions of Bantock's recent book. See BANTOCK, G.H. (1980) *Dilemmas of the Curriculum*, Oxford, Martin Robertson.

26 Schools Council (1982) *Multicultural Education*, London, March, p. 6.

27 Schools Council (1981) 'Programmes of work: Programme five — Improving the examinations system: Appendix E(18) — Assessment in a multicultural society', London, Schools Council, p. 1, cyclo.

28 See *The Guardian*, 26 October 1982; *The Times Educational Supplement*, 29 October 1982, 19 November 1982, 3 December 1982; GILL, D. (1982) 'Geography for the young school leaver: A critique and secondary school geography in London: An assessment of its contribution to multicultural education', London, Centre for Multicultural Education, University of London Institute of Education, and 'Assessment in a multicultural society: Schools Council report: Geography', cyclo, unpublished document.

29 NUTTALL, D. (1979) 'The myth of comparability', *Journal of the Association of Inspectors and Educational Advisers*, Autumn, pp. 16–18.

30 CRAFT, M. (1982) *Education for Diversity: The Challenge of Cultural Pluralism*, University of Nottingham, p. 22.

31 At the time of writing the Department of Industry was still engaged in drawing up an agreed Code of Practice on the Employment of Ethnic Minority Personnel. This has now been published by the Commission for Racial Equality (1983).

32 I do not propose to repeat here the definition of the underlying ethic and social imperatives which may underlie such guidelines. See LYNCH, J. (1983) *op. cit.*

33 I am grateful to Professor James Banks for a copy of an unpublished paper on this issue. BANKS, J.A. (1981) 'Social problems and educational equity in the eighties', United States Department of Education, School Finance Project, August.

34 TROYNA, B. (1983) 'Multicultural education: Emancipation or containment', unpublished paper presented at the Sociology of Education Conference, Westhill College, Birmingham, 3–5 January.

35 A similar point is made by two advocates of recurrent education. See FLUDE, R. and PARROTT, A. (1980) 'Memorials to past problems', *The Times Educational Supplement*, 28 November, p. 4.

Intercultural Relations in the Classroom

Ken Thomas

This chapter considers the intercultural perceptions and attitudes of schoolchildren, an area of increasing significance in educational and social policy, and presents a critical review of relevant research studies.

Social attitudes may be seen as means of simplifying the environment by providing us with pre-set styles of response in given situations. They supply general guides to behaviour so that we do not have to appraise anew every social situation in which we find ourselves. This is not to say that attitudes determine our behaviour in an entirely predictable way, as behaviour in any situation will depend on a variety of psychological and situational variables. But attitudes do predispose us to behave in certain ways and so allow a certain economy of effort.

Attitudes are not innate, but are acquired through social experience and are generally regarded as being comprised of three elements: a knowledge component, a feeling component, and a behavioural component. The process of attitude formation is seen as a matter of increasing differentiation with age in each of these components. In the process of socialization, intergroup attitudes begin to form as the child gradually acquires the beliefs held about different groups, together with the feelings aroused and the behaviours usually adopted towards them by members of his own group. This is a gradual and complex process, and one in which the two overlapping stages of awareness and orientation are seen to precede the development of true adult-like attitudes (Harding *et al.*, 1969).

Awareness

A fundamental ingredient in the development of an intergroup attitude is the ability to recognize differences between people. A prerequisite in the development of this ability is that the child must first be able to differentiate 'self' from others. Child psychologists are agreed that the development of a full awareness of 'self' is not innate, but as Piaget (1930) observed, 'the result of progressive dissociation and not a primitive intuition' (p. 128).

This process of dissociation begins with the maturation of the physical senses and the growing ability of the child to differentiate between 'me' and 'not me' objects. One of the distinctions the child is gradually able to make is that some people are 'like me' and others 'not like me'. The ability to make this distinction depends on the development of perceptual skills, and can be achieved without verbal instruction. It therefore seems surprising that the view that 'young children are often unconscious of skin colour differences' should be still heard in school staffrooms. This view is not only contradicted by common sense, but also by a good deal of research evidence which shows that children may be aware of skin-colour differences as early as three years of age, with increasing awareness thereafter (Clark and Clark, 1947; Goodman, 1952; Landreth and Johnson, 1953; Morland, 1958; Vaughan, 1963).

With the development of perceptual skills comes an increase in social awareness. At the same time the child becomes increasingly able to verbalize what is seen. The range of personal contact widens, and so the child is more apt to notice differences and to have differences brought to his or her attention. Thus by the age of 5 or 6 most children demonstrate a full awareness of skin-colour, or obvious racial differences between groups.

Ethnicity, on the other hand, is a more complex concept than race. It 'refers to characteristics of groups that may be [present] in different proportions, physical, national, cultural, linguistic or ideological in character. Unlike "race" the term does not imply biological unity' (Allport, 1954, preface). The development of an awareness of ethnic differences therefore requires more than the development of perceptual skills. The ability to place 'self' and 'others' by religion or nationality, for example, involves complex and abstract categorization that can only be based on personal experience to a limited extent. It should therefore be expected that ethnic awareness develops later than race awareness, and research evidence indicates that this is, indeed, the case (Hartley *et al.*, 1948; Radke, *et al.*, 1949; Piaget and Weil, 1951; Jahoda, 1962; Tajfel *et al.*, 1970). A concept such as 'nation', for example, appears to be highly confused for most children at the age of 6 or 7. Not until the ages of 10 or 11 do children appear to grasp adult-type concepts of 'nationality' with a full understanding of the concepts of 'home country' and 'foreign'.

Orientation

Following the initial recognition of differences between people, there comes a gradual belief in the significance of these differences. The child begins to learn the words and phrases commonly used within his own group to describe members of other groups. Many of these words and phrases will have an evaluative orientation and involve the attribution of supposed traits to other groups. Thus as the child is socialized into the beliefs and values of his own groups and comes to accept them as 'normal', the behaviours and beliefs of other groups come to be seen as 'abnormal'. This may be seen as ethnocentrism (a generalized attitude of preference for one's own group) in its most naive form. Segall *et al.* (1966) described this as 'phenomenal absolutism', a mode of thinking whereby the individual unreflectively takes his own group's values as objective reality, and uses them as the context within which he judges less familiar objects and events. It simply does not occur to the individual that there may be other explanations or more than one point of view.

Ethnocentrism, however, involves more than just intellectual functioning. It is a generalized attitude, and as such involves both positive and negative 'feelings'. Gradually these feelings of belonging might become such that the symbols and values of one's own group become the objects of attachment and pride, while the symbols and values of other groups become the objects of contempt and hatred. Ethnocentrism in this form may be seen as 'a generalized attitude which predisposes an individual to reject members of groups other than his own and to exalt the superiority of his own group, especially his ethnic and national groups' (Kretch *et al.*, 1962, p. 75); it is this basic attitude which underlies the use of race prejudice as a weapon in group conflict.

A number of researchers have emphasized the importance of early socializing forces in the development of negative intergroup attitudes. In the process of socialization there occurs what Van den Berghe (1970) described as the necessary conjunction of objective and subjective conditions which give race and ethnicity social significance. The subjective perceptions (popular beliefs about 'own' and 'other' groups) 'crystallize around clusters of objective characteristics (increasing awareness of racial and ethnic differences) that become badges of inclusion and exclusion' (*op. cit.*, p. xviii). In the transmission of these 'popular beliefs' it is not surprising that the role of parents has been found to be of central importance (Horowitz and Horowitz, 1938; Allport and Kramer, 1968; Radke-Yarrow *et al.*, 1952; Mosher and Scodel, 1960; Pushkin, 1967; Marsh, 1970). Gradually, as these popular beliefs are learned, stereotypes begin to form.

The term 'stereotype' was first introduced by Lippman (1922) who saw it as part of a simplifying mechanism to handle 'the real environment which is altogether too big, too complex and too fleeting for direct acquaintance' (p. 16). A distinction must, however, be made between the universal tendency to categorize, as a means of simplifying the environment, and the process of stereotyping. As Allport (1954) pointed out:

> a stereotype is not identical with a category; it is rather a fixed idea that accompanies a category. For example, the category 'Negro' can be held in mind simply as a neutral, factual, non-evaluative concept, pertaining merely to racial stock. Stereotype enters when, and if, the initial category is freighted with 'pictures' and judgements of the Negro as musical, lazy, superstitious, or what not (p. 187).

Once formed, the stereotype influences the perceptual and judgemental processes so that differences between groups are exaggerated while differences within groups are minimized. Reaction is then not to a particular individual but to the stereotype of the racial or ethnic group with which that individual has been identified. When this identification is made the whole range of beliefs held about the group are automatically ascribed to the individual.

Own-Group Rejection

It has been argued (for example, Milner, 1975; Bagley and Coard, 1975) that in a predominantly white-oriented society such as Great Britain, the popular stereotypes encountered by the black or white child, as each proceeds through this stage of orientation, are quite different. The own-group stereotypes encountered by the white child, it is argued, are essentially favourable, while the own-group stereotypes encountered by the black child are essentially derogatory. As a consequence, it is suggested, many black children may internalize these derogatory stereotypes and develop negative attitudes toward their own-race groups.

Evidence of this own-group rejection has been provided by a number of researchers who have studied young children's preferences for dolls representing different race groups. This method has been frequently used in the study of the race group orientations of very young children, as the techniques of attitude assessment more usually used with older children and adults are inappropriate. The child is presented with a number of dolls representing various race groups, and is asked to select the doll preferred in a variety of situations. This choice is then taken as an indication of the child's attitude.

One outstandingly consistent finding of the majority of studies of young children's preferences in this context has been that both black and white children tend to express preferences for white dolls and figures. This is a finding not only of studies of Negro and white children in America (Clark and Clark 1947; Goodman, 1952; Landreth and Johnson, 1953; Morland, 1958; Stevenson and Stewart, 1958), but also of studies of Oriental and white children in Hawaii (Springer, 1950), Maori and white children in New Zealand (Vaughan, 1963; 1964) and West Indian and white children in England (Milner, 1970; Davey and Norburn, 1980).

However, growing doubt has been cast on these findings and conclusions over recent years. One of the major areas of concern centres on the validity and reliability of the measure. When presented with a number of dolls and asked to choose from them, a child's selection might be influenced by a treasured doll already owned, in which case the test would simply be a measure of response-set, and invalid as a measure of race attitude. Katz and Zalk (1974), for example, presented children with dolls that differed only in skin colour; that is, both black and white dolls had brown eyes and dark brown hair. In these conditions the strong preference for white dolls found in other studies was not obtained. Richardson and Green (1971) also emphasized the importance of perceptual cues other than skin-colour in influencing children's preferences.

Porter (1971) advanced the argument that the selections made by children in many studies could well have been influenced by the race of the investigator. As most of the investigators will have been white, it is suggested that children may have chosen the white doll in order to be friendly to the white investigator. There is evidence that in a variety of research settings children's preferences may be influenced in the direction of greater favourability toward the race group of the investigator (Trent, 1954; Kraus, 1962; Vaughan, 1964b; Summers and Hammond, 1966; Katz and Zalk, 1974; Thomas, 1982).

Katz and Zalk (1974) have further pointed out that it has never been shown that young children's doll preferences are consistent over time. In the only attempt to relate these preferences to actual intergroup behaviour, Hraba and Grant (1970) could find no such relationship.

The contradictions in these findings may be explained by the poor psychometric characteristics of the measures used. However, the evidence of self-group rejection in black pupils generally is also contradictory, with the earlier researchers tending to find such rejection while the later studies do not (Milner, 1983). Coopersmith (1975), for example, concluded a review of the American evidence on self-esteem in black students with the observation that earlier trends for black students to have lower self-esteem than whites appeared to have been reversed. Similarly, D'Souza (1978) and Thomas (1981) in studies of British adolescents found no evidence that black pupils either rejected their own-race groups, or attributed more favourable characteristics to white groups, in the way described by Bagley and Coard (1975). Indeed, in his study of the stereotypes held by English, West Indian, Indian and Pakistani pupils, Thomas noted how each group saw itself in overwhelmingly favourable terms.

The contradictions in these findings may possibly be explained by a changed perspective on the part of black people over recent years, i.e. that the denial of full acceptance and equality of opportunity within society is now seen for what it is — a social and political failure and not an individual failure. Another, but not entirely inconsistent possibility, concerns the particular social climates within which the various studies have been carried out. Coopersmith (1975) argued that a social environment which insulated black children from 'direct assaults upon their feelings ... [provided] the support to reject the low status to which white society assigns them' (pp. 161–2). Similarly, Bagley *et al.* (1979) concluded, from a review of the British literature on self-esteem, that the findings seemed 'to support the American research which has shown that the social context of the school and the degree to which it insulates pupils from the demeaning forces of racism is an important influence on self-esteem' (p. 189).

Thus it is possible that the contradictions in the findings may be explained by the extent to which teachers, and others, have been able to foster social climates which counter what, in other circumstances, might be tendencies to internalize negative stereotypes.

Sociometric Studies of Race and Ethnic Orientation

Sociometric methodology has been used fairly extensively in the study of children's race and ethnic orientations from about the age of 5 onwards. Within the field the most popular procedure has undoubtedly been the sociometric nomination technique. This technique requires children to nominate those classmates they regard as best friends or who they would choose as partners on specified activities. Statistical analysis (see Criswell, 1939) may then be undertaken to determine the extent to which these preferences are influenced by group membership. Applied in this manner, the technique has been used to provide an attitude measure with essentially a behavioural orientation.

Adopting this procedure, researchers in both America (Criswell, 1939; Koch, 1946; Shaw, 1975) and Britain (Rowley, 1967; Durojaiye, 1969; Aslin, 1970) have reported that, at least up to the stage of early adolescence, black children appear to be more out-group oriented than whites. At a superficial level, these findings could be taken to support the view that black children tend to reject their own group. Yet from the earliest studies of Moreno (1934) and Criswell (1937; 1939) to the more recent studies of Shaw (1973) and Gerard *et al.* (1975), American researchers have consistently demonstrated that in most choice situations, *children express preference for members of their own race group*. It could be argued that as the aims of the majority of American researchers have been to examine the effects of segregated or desegregated schooling on children's cross-race relationships, this should not be surprising. But the evidence from studies carried out in this country indicates that the friendship preferences of children in British Schools are similarly influenced (Kawwa, 1965, 1968; Rowley, 1967; Durojaiye, 1969; Robertson and Kawwa, 1971; Thomas, 1975).

The apparent out-group orientation of black children should therefore be seen quite simply as differing degrees of strength of in-group orientation. This view is supported by the findings of Shaw (1975), one of the few researchers to study rejection as well as preference patterns. An examination of preference patterns revealed that in-group preference was stronger in white children than in black. But examination of the rejection patterns failed to find any evidence that black children were rejecting their own group.

Further, the evidence is by no means consistent. Several researchers have reported that in-group preference in black pre-adolescent children is *stronger* than in white (Gerard *et al.*, 1975; Kawwa, 1968; Hartley, 1970). It is therefore important to recognize that the investigation of both intra and intergroup attitude formation is far from complete. The questions raised regarding the validity and reliability of studies of very young children, and the contradictory evidence from the sociometric studies, indicate both the complex nature of the area under study and the need to treat these findings with caution.

Intergroup Attitude Development in Older Children

It is generally assumed that as the child gradually learns his group's repertoire of responses towards members of other groups, those responses the individual considers appropriate for himself become integrated so that a self-consistent pattern emerges (Horowitz, 1936; Wilson, 1963; Vaughan, 1964c). Several investigators have reported that in this process there is a tendency for the level of intergroup prejudice to increase as children grow older, before levelling off at some point in adolescence (Minard, 1931; Horowitz, 1936; Vaughan and Thompson, 1961).

In the investigation of the development of intergroup attitudes through this period, sociometric techniques have been fairly widely used. These techniques have been favoured on the grounds that the measures may well tap children's beliefs and feelings about other groups, as well as their behavioural intentions with regard to individual members of those groups. The peer-nomination technique, described earlier, has been the method used in the vast majority of studies.

Moreno (1934), in pioneering the technique, was the first investigator to report that preference for own-race group increased with age. In a study of black and white elementary school children, it was reported that cleavage between the two groups did not occur to any significant extent before the age of 9, but then increased to reach a peak at the age of 11. Criswell's (1937, 1939) findings were similar. Radke et al. (1950) reported that cleavage between the two race groups did not occur until the age of 11, but then preference for own-group increased in strength to the age of 14. The findings of Bartel et al. (1973) were similar.

Koch (1946) reported differences in the groups under study. Over the extended age-range of 8 to 18, evidence of white in-group preference was found at 8, and this rose in strength to the age of 16. On the other hand, while there was little evidence of black in-group preference at the age of 8, by the age of 14 it had become very strong.

In a short-term longitudinal study of black and white children in one elementary school, Shaw (1973) reported that while all friendship choices were strongly influenced by race there was no evidence of an increase in follow-up testing after intervals of four and twelve months. This is, however, a relatively short space of time over which to expect such changes to occur. Gerard *et al.* (1975), in a more extensive longitudinal study over a six-year period, found that own-race group friendship choices predominated and that this own-group preference increased with age.

Increasing preference for own-race group with age has been a fairly consistent finding of American research studies and similar findings have been reported in Britain. This is particularly so where the extended age-range into adolescence has been studied. Here, the same tendency for preference for own-race group to increase with age has been reported.

Rushton (1967), in a small-scale survey of white, West Indian and Asian children aged between 8 and 15, reported that cleavage between the groups occurred at about the age of 11 with a slight increase in own-group preference thereafter. Rowley (1967), in a study of 1747 white, West Indian and Indian children's preferences, similarly reported a slight tendency for in-group preference to increase with age.

Robertson and Kawwa (1971) studied the friendship preferences of 604 white, West Indian and Asian pupils in a girls' comprehensive secondary school. It was reported that children preferred to choose friends from their own-race groups, and this effect was most apparent in the choices of the older pupils. Thomas (1975) investigated the friendship choices of 475 white, West Indian, and Cypriot pupils aged between 11 and 15 in a boys' secondary school. Strong in-group preference was reported in all groups at all ages, and this preference was strongest in the 15-year-old group.

By far the most extensive study of intergroup relations in British schools was that carried out by Jelinek and Brittan (1975). As part of a larger study of pupils in multiracial schools, the friendship patterns of a national sample of 677 8-year-old, 611 10-year-old, and 1507 12-year-old boys and girls were examined. Subjects were asked to nominate three best friends at school (actual friendships), and the three children they would most like as friends (desired friendships). Criswell self-preference indices (Criswell, 1939) were then calculated for each of the major sub-groups represented within each of these age-groups. These were defined as pupils of white British, West Indian and Asian origin. Analysis of both actual and desired friendship choices revealed that at all ages own-group preference was demonstrated, to the extent that Jelinek and Brittan commented, 'perhaps the most striking findings of this study concerned the low level of inter-ethnic friendships — or phrased differently, the high degree of own-group preferences' (p. 51). It was also reported that in both actual and desired friendships, this own-group preference increased with age.

However, there is one major, often unacknowledged, potential source of bias in the peer-nomination technique when applied in this manner. In most studies each child is asked to nominate a limited number of companions according to specified criteria. Yet it is possible that children generally accept their cross-race peers without choosing them in any of these categories. As a consequence, an unduly negative picture of children's cross-race relationships could be presented in studies where choice restrictions have been imposed.

If we take Criswell's study, for example, subjects were asked to name two boys or two girls they would like to sit by in school. Criswell recognized the inherent problem of such choice restriction when she stated that her results were 'specific to the strongest attractions which each individual feels for other individuals. Third or fourth choices might yield other findings' (p. 18). An alternative sociometric measure which to a large extent overcomes the problem of bias has been applied in a few more recent studies with quite interesting results.

Sociometric 'Roster-and-Rating' Studies

The basic format of this technique is similar to the Ohio Social Acceptance Scale (Raths, 1943, 1947) and the Classroom Social Distance Scale (Cunningham, 1951), two other fairly widely used measures of children's social preference patterns. Each child is presented with an alphabetically ordered class roster, and asked to rate (usually on a five-point scale) each of the other class members according to specified criteria. These ratings are then averaged to provide indices of popularity with (average of ratings received), and friendliness towards (average of ratings given), each of the sub-groups identified in the classroom.

The results of studies where this type of procedure has been used (e.g. Raths and Schweikart, 1946; Singleton et al., 1976; St. John and Lewis, 1975; Singleton and Asher, 1977; Thomas, 1981) indicate a more positive picture of interracial association than that found in peer-nomination studies. Although the influence of race, which increased with age, was apparent in the ratings in each of these studies 'the degree of bias was small compared to that obtained in studies using friendship nomination sociometric measures' (Singleton and Asher, p. 10). The children in these studies did not appear to be drastically isolated from each other, even though they did prefer members of their own-race groups as friends. It therefore seems possible that when children are given the opportunity to rate *all* of their classmates, no forced choices are required and there is less race bias as a result.

A further consideration here concerns the continuing ethical problem in sociometric research of the use of negative criteria. If asking children to nominate those they would least like as friends or associates results in some being made more conscious of feelings of rejection, then, as Gronlund (1959) argued, 'neither the emotional development of the individual nor the social development of the group will be benefited' (p. 47). Nevertheless, Gronlund went on to point out that 'detecting unexpressed feelings of rejection might be needed in the evaluation of attempts to integrate minority group members' (p. 47).

This is an important consideration, as few researchers have examined rejection patterns. The assumption has been that increasing preference for own-race group automatically implies increasing rejection of the other group. To the extent that the majority of researchers have used the peer-nomination technique the assumption is probably valid. With increasing age there appears to be a reordering of friendship preference with the highest level choices becoming more racially homogeneous. But as already pointed out, the use of this particular technique may in fact heighten apparent cleavage between race-groups and fail to reveal more subtle changes in children's friendship patterns.

Age and Intra-Group Relationships

One of the advantages of the roster-and-rating procedure is that it allows a close examination of changes in friendship tendencies towards other race-groups. It is surprising that the majority of researchers who have used this procedure have not given greater consideration to this dimension, as these particular findings could critically influence the ways in which the evidence of age-related patterns of own-race group preference is interpreted. The need for such consideration was emphasized by the findings of a recent study (Thomas, 1981) in which both own-race group and other-race group friendship patterns were examined.

The aspect of the study relevant here concerns the influence of race on the friendship ratings of all the pupils of English (208 boys, 190 girls) and West Indian (133 boys, 117 girls) origin, on the roll of an East Midlands comprehensive school. The particular roster-and-rating technique used was similar to that designed by Lewis (1971) to overcome the problem of the use of negative criteria. Alphabetically arranged class lists were handed to the pupils who were asked to: 'Put a 1 by the names of all your *very best* friends in the class; put a 2 by the names of your good friends (not *best* friends, just *good* friends); put a 3 by the names of those who are not your friends but who you feel are okay; then put a 4 by the names of all those you don't know very well.'

Using this procedure some names remain unnumbered, and these were later assigned a 5 on the grounds that they were the most ignored, or least liked, pupils in the classroom.

These ratings were then averaged to create indices of friendliness toward English boys, West Indian boys, English girls, and West Indian girls, respectively.

The initial comparisons of these mean ratings revealed several interesting findings. First, that the influence of sex was a more important determining factor on the ratings given by all pupils than the influence of race. This finding is, of course, consistent with those of other studies where the influence of race and sex has been compared. Secondly, while race was a more influential determining factor on the ratings given by the West Indian pupils than by the English pupils, the vast majority of all same-sex ratings were between two and three, or, between being 'a good friend' and 'okay'. Thus the procedure revealed a degree of cross-racial social acceptance that would not have been shown by the sociometric peer-nomination technique. Thirdly, it was apparent that the most friendly same-sex ratings were not given by the oldest pupils, but by those pupils aged 12 or 13. The English patterns showed an increase in friendliness to this age which was followed by a gradual decline. The West Indian patterns showed an increase in friendliness to about the same age, followed by a sharp decline before a gradual increase again to the age of 16.

To this extent, the study was similar to several other studies where developmental implications have been drawn from cross-age group samples. However, it differed from most others in that a longitudinal study was carried out in order to further investigate the apparent peak in friendliness at the age of 12 or 13.

A sub-sample of forty English (twenty boys, twenty girls) and thirty-two West Indian (nineteen boys, thirteen girls) first year pupils; and forty-seven English (twenty-six boys, twenty-one girls) and forty-one West Indian (twenty-five boys, sixteen girls) was retested after an interval of two years. The analysis of changes in the ratings over the two-year period revealed similar patterns to those shown in the cross-age group analysis. Over time there appeared to be an increase in same-sex own-race group friendliness, to about the age of 13, which was followed by a gradual decrease. The tentative conclusion was drawn that the relationship between age and intra-group friendliness could well be curvilinear, with a maximum at 13 or 14.

Age and Inter-group Relationships

However, how this finding is interpreted must depend on the relationship of age to intergroup friendship tendencies. To what extent can it be assumed that increasing intragroup friendliness *automatically* implies lessening intergroup friendliness? This is a question that the sociometric roster-and-rating procedure allows us to at least begin to answer.

It has already been pointed out that the cross-year group analysis showed very similar age-related patterns of same-sex and own-race and same-sex other-race ratings. The longitudinal analysis revealed that this was also the case with the ratings of the year two pupils. Over the two-year period, both same-sex own-race and same-sex other-race ratings changed in a less friendly direction. However, the ratings of the first year pupils changed in opposite directions. The same-sex own-race ratings became more friendly, while the same-sex other-race ratings became less friendly.

On the basis of this evidence, it was then suggested that it seemed possible that the age-related patterns of friendship tendencies towards classmates of both own and other-race group could well fellow similar curves. An increase in friendliness toward own-race group classmates might, in certain circumstances, be *accompanied* by an increase in friendliness towards other-race classmates, although the maximum of the friendliness curve of any specific racial or ethnic group, and the degree of cleavage between that group and any other, will vary according to the particular social climate in which the study was carried out. Certainly, in this particular study features of the school's internal climate were identified which made it atypical of many inner-city multiracial schools.

Some Influences on the Development of Inter-Group Relationships

This explanation would fit well with Wilson's (1963) suggestion that a negatively accelerated growth curve provided a general model for the development of prejudice in childhood and adolescence. That is, the general level of prejudice increases, but at a declining rate until it stabilizes at the adult level. Both the within and between-group variations in terms of the age at which race cleavage first appears and later peaks in strength is explained by the different *social influences and experiences* the subjects of the various studies have been exposed to. Some of these influences will have promoted, while others will have delayed, the development of prejudice and in-group tendencies. Thus different groups may manifest similarly shaped growth curves, yet one may develop earlier than another.

Gronlund (1959) also thought that differences in the degree of cleavage between race groups found in the literature could be accounted for by situational circumstances. He pointed out that the distinct cleavage between black and white children reported by Moreno (1934) and Criswell (1937, 1939) could be related to the fact that these studies were carried out in large metropolitan areas at a time when segregation was common. In support of this point of view, Gronlund quoted the Raths and Schweikart (1946) study where cleavage between race groups was not as apparent. He suggested that this was due to the fact that integration had been in effect for a period of years in the area in which the study was carried out.

This view would be consistent with Homans' (1950) empirical generalization that the more frequently people interact, the stronger their friendship sentiments are likely to be. While there will obviously be exceptions, for example, people of conflicting temperaments may well not get along together, the hypothesis does fit in with common sense and was supported initially by Homans' theoretical analysis of five group studies carried out by other researchers. Other researchers have since provided evidence to support the proposition. For example, Hallinan (1976) and Felmlee and Hallinan (1979) reported that friendship choices were more evenly distributed, with less evidence of clique formation in classrooms where the organizational structures allowed a high level of interaction amongst pupils.

The organizational structures of the school may also impose limitations on the opportunities for interaction amongst pupils that can have profound implications for the formation and maintenance of friendship groups. Hargreaves (1967) and Lacey (1970), for example, each studied the effects of streaming on group formation in all white secondary schools. Hargreaves noted the way in which the initial division of pupils into streams restricted opportunities for interaction between pupils from different streams. As a consequence of this process, the particular stream to which a pupil was allocated became a major influence on friendship formation. Over a period of four years, the social distance between pupils in the top and bottom streams became so large that Hargreaves argued it was possible to identify two quite distinct and powerful subcultural groupings with few channels of communication between. There developed in the top stream a subculture, which he termed the 'academic', with norms and values that were, in essence, extensions of those of the school. The subculture which developed in the bottom stream was termed 'delinquescent'. Here the dominant norms and values tended to be the inverse of those of the school, with delinquent acts being necessary to achieve high status within the peer group.

These studies have serious implications for teachers in multiracial schools, for as a number of researchers have noted (Bhatnagar, 1970; Kawwa and Robertson, 1971; Thomas, 1975), a consequence of streaming in such schools can mean that black children tend to be overrepresented in the bottom streams and underrepresented in the top streams. If the same processes identified by Hargreaves and Lacey operate in this setting, there is the possibility that the organizational structure of the school will impose limitations on opportunities for interaction between groups that may be racially based. This may lead not only to increased social cleavage between race-groups, but also to the development of a predominantly black subculture within which those pupils who lack success, in the terms of the school, become progressively alienated from it.

Driver (1977) produced evidence to suggest that this was more than just a possibility. In a study of black and white pupils in one West Midlands secondary school, he found that the process of selection and streaming created social environments with different racial characteristics. Purposive academic and socially prestigious activities among the top-stream pupils tended to emphasize their personal qualities and de-emphasize their intraracial loyalties. The bottom stream pupils, on the other hand, felt much less positively about themselves and the importance of their school activities, and formed friendship groups almost exclusively with members of their own-race groups.

Similarly Troyna (1978), in a study of the social relationships of 15-year-old pupils in a rigidly streamed multiracial school, reported that the degree of intraracial group commitment was stronger in the bottom streams than the top streams. This was particularly so amongst the black pupils who had immersed themselves in racially exclusive friendship groups. Troyna interpreted this finding in the wider social context. He argued that the withdrawal of the black pupils in the bottom streams into racially exclusive friendship groups resulted from a 'realisation of a common identity and shared destiny. These are the pupils who are most vulnerable to unemployment, police confrontations and other manifestations of normative racism in contemporary Britain. This realisation serves to differentiate them not only from the black pupils in the higher streams but also from their classmates' (p. 64). Teachers should therefore be aware that the internal organization of the school, and in particular its grouping and streaming policy, gives off signals to the pupil. The pupil will respond to these signals according to the frame of reference brought to the situation. Where schools, far from 'insulating pupils from the de-meaning forces of racism' are seen, through their organizational structures, to mirror and reinforce the divisions and inequalities that exist within society, then a consequence might be that they will become 'arenas for the expression of frustrations felt by both white and black, and the resulting hostility and conflict is demoralising for both groups' (Bagley *et al.*, 1979, p. 189).

However, despite the problem of racial discrimination in the wider society, and in particular the evidence of discrimination faced by young black school leavers (Hubbock and Carter, 1980), it could be argued, as suggested earlier, that some schools have achieved what Bagley *et al.* described as 'true integration'. True integration refers to a social climate within which there 'are cross-racial friendships, racial interdependence, and a strong measure of personal autonomy' (p. 189). While policymakers at national and local levels seem unable to effectively counter racism in society, it is possible that some schools may be fostering greater understanding and mutual acceptance.

Finally, it must again be stated that the investigation of both intra and intergroup attitude formation is far from complete. Hartup (1970) argued that there was 'a desperate need for integrative theorizing' (p. 364) in the area of children's peer relations in general; and our discussion here leads to the conclusion that this is particularly so in the area of children's intercultural relations. In attempting to trace the course of race and ethnic attitude formation, this discussion has led to the identification of several methodological and interpretive difficulties. It has, for example, been shown that the use of a particular sociometric technique which provides only a partial picture of children's intercultural relations, and the partial interpretation of the results of procedures that provide more complete pictures, may result in an exaggeration of the extent to which these relations are influenced by race.

Thus there is a clear need for further developmental research and integrative theorizing. This research should also include attempts to identify the institutional forces which might promote or prevent true integration.

References

ALLPORT, G.W. and KRAMER, B.M. (1946) 'Some roots or prejudice', *Journal of Psychology*, 22, pp. 9–39.

ALLPORT, G.W. (1954) *The Nature of Prejudice*, Boston, Mass., Addison-Wesley.

ASLIN, R.E. (1970) *A Comparative Sociometric Study of the Social Integration of Coloured Immigrant Children in a Junior School*, unpublished DipEd dissertation, Institute of Education, University of Nottingham.

BAGLEY, C. and COARD, B. (1975) 'Cultural knowledge and rejection of ethnic identity in West Indian children in London', in VERMA, G.K. and BAGLEY, C. (Eds) *Race and Education Across Cultures*, London, Heinemann, pp. 322–31.

BAGLEY, C., *et al.* (1979) 'Pupil self-esteem: A study of black and white teenagers in British schools', in VERMA, G.K. and BAGLEY, C. (Eds) *Race Education and Identity*, London, Macmillan, pp. 176–91.

BHATNAGAR, J. (1970) *Immigrants at School*, London, Cornmarket Press.

CLARK, K.B. and CLARK, M.P. (1947) 'Racial identification and preference in children', in NEWCOMB, T.M. and HARTLEY, E.L. (Eds), *Readings in Social Psychology*, New York, Holt.

COOPERSMITH, S. (1975) 'Self-concept, race and education', in VERMA, G.K. and BAGLEY, C. (Eds) *Race and Education across Cultures*, London, Heinemann.

CRISWELL, J.H. (1937) 'Racial cleavage in Negro-white groups', *Sociometry*, 1, pp. 81–9.

CRISWELL, J.H. (1939) 'A sociometric study of race cleavage in the classroom', *Archives of Psychology*, 235, pp. 1–82.

CUNNINGHAM, R. (1951) *Understanding Group Behaviour of Boys and Girls*, Columbia, Teachers College, Columbia University.

DAVEY, A.G. and NORBURN, (1980) 'Ethnic awareness and ethnic differentiation amongst primary school children', *New Community*, 3, pp. 51–60.

DRIVER, G. (1977) 'Cultural competence, social power and school achievement: A case study of West Indians attending a secondary school in the West Midlands', *New Community*, 5, pp. 353–9.

D'SOUZA, M.B. (1978) 'Intergroup attitudes in multi-ethnic schools', *Oxford Review of Education*, 4, 2, pp. 149–60.

DUROJAIYE, M.O.A. (1969) 'Race relations among Junior school children', *Educational Research*, 11, pp. 226–8.

FELMLEE, D. and HALLINAN, M.T. (1979) 'The effect of classroom interaction on children's friendships', *Journal of Classroom Interaction*, 14, 2, Summer, pp. 1–8.

GERARD, H.B., *et al.* (1975) 'Social contact in the desegregated classroom', in GERARD, H.B. and MILLER, N. (Eds) *School Desegregation*, New York, Plenum.

GOODMAN, M.E. (1952) *Race Awareness in Young Children*, Cambridge, Mass., Addison-Wesley.

GRONLUND, N.E. (1959) *Sociometry in the Classroom*, New York, Harper and Brothers.

HALLINAN, M.T. (1976) 'Friendship patterns in open and traditional classrooms', *Sociology of Education*, 49, October, pp. 254–65.

HARDING, J., *et al.* (1969) 'Prejudice and ethnic relations', in LINDZEY, G. and ARONSON, E. (Eds), *The Handbook of Social Psychology*, New York, Addison-Wesley.

HARGREAVES, D.H. (1967) *Social Relations in a Secondary School*, London, Routledge and Kegan Paul.

HARTLEY, E.L., *et al.* (1948) 'Children's use of ethnic frames of reference: An exploratory study of children's conceptualization of multiple ethnic group membership', *Journal of Psychology*, 26, pp. 367–8.

HARTUP, W.W. (1970) 'Peer interaction and social organisation', in MUSSEN, P.H. (Ed.), *Carmichael's Manual of Child Psychology*, Vol. 2, pp. 361–456, New York, John Wiley.

HOMANS, G.C. (1950) *The Human Group*, New York, Harcourt.

HOROWITZ, E.L. (1936) 'Development of attitude toward Negroes', *Archives of Psychology*, No. 194.

HOROWITZ, E.L. and HOROWITZ, R.E. (1938) 'Development of social attitudes in children', *Sociometry*, 1, pp. 307–38.

HRABA, J. and GRANT, G. (1970) 'Black is beautiful: A re-examination of racial preference and identity', *Journal of Clinical and Social Psychology*, 16, pp. 398–402.

HUBBUCK, J. and CARTER, S. (1980) *Half a Chance? A Report on Job Discrimination Against Young Blacks in Nottingham*, London, CRE.

JAHODA, G. (1962) 'Development of Scottish children's ideas and attitudes about other countries', *Journal of Social Psychology*, 58, pp. 91–108.

JELINEK, M.M. and BRITTAN, E.M. (1975) 'Multiracial Education 1. Interethnic friendship patterns', *Educational Research* 18, 1, pp. 44–53.

KATZ, P.A. and ZALK, S.R. (1974) 'Doll preferences: An index of racial attitudes', *Journal of Educational Psychology*, 66, 5, pp. 663–8.

KAWWA, T. (1965) *A Study of the Interaction between Native and Immigrant Children in English Schools with Special Reference to Ethnic Prejudice*, unpublished PhD thesis, Institute of Education, University of London.

KAWWA, T. (1968) 'Three sociometric studies of ethnic relations in London schools', *British Journal of Social and Clinical Psychology*, 7.

KOCH, H.L. (1946) 'The social distance test between certain racial, nationality and skin-pigmentation groups in selected populations of American schoolchildren', *Journal of General Psychology*, 68, pp. 63–95.

KRAUS, S. (1962) 'Modifying prejudice: Attitude change as a function of race of the communicator', *Audio-visual Communication Review*, 10, pp. 14–22.

KRETCH, D., et al. (1962) *Individual in Society*, New York, McGraw-Hill.

LACEY, C. (1970) *Hightown Grammar*, Manchester, Manchester University Press.

LANDRETH, C. and JOHNSON, B.C. (1953) 'Young children's responses to a picture and inset test designed to reveal reactions to persons of different skin colour', *Child Development*, 24, pp. 63–80.

LEWIS, R.G. (1971) *The Relationship of Classroom Racial Composition to Student Academic Achievement and the Conditioning Effects of Interracial Social Acceptance*, unpublished EdD dissertation, Harvard University.

LIPPMAN, R. (1922) *Public Opinion*, New York, Harcourt-Brace.

MARSH, A. (1970) 'Awareness of racial differences in *West African* and British children', *Race*, 3, pp. 289–302.

MILNER, D. (1970) *Ethnic Identity and Preference in Minority-Group Children*, unpublished PhD thesis, Faculty of Social Science, University of Bristol.

MILNER, D. (1975) *Children and Race*, Harmondsworth, Penguin.

MILNER, D. (1983) *Children and Race: Ten Years On*, London, Ward Lock Educational.

MINARD, R.D. (1931) 'Race attitudes of Iowa children', *University of Iowa Studies Characteristics*, 4, 2.

MORENO, J.L. (1934) *Who Shall Survive?* Washington, D.C., Nervous and Mental Disease Pub. Co.

MORLAND, J.K. (1958) 'Racial recognition by nursery school children in Lynchburg, Virginia', *Social Forces*, 37, pp. 132–7.

MOSHER, D.L. and SCODEL, A. (1960) 'Relationship between ethnocentrism in children and the ethnocentrism and child rearing practices of their mothers', *Child Development*, 31, pp. 369–76.

PIAGET, J. (1930) *The Child's Conception of Causality*, London, Routledge and Kegan Paul.

PIAGET, J. and WEIL, A. (1951) 'The development in children of an idea of homeland and relations with other countries', *International Social Science Bulletin*, 3, pp. 561–78.

PORTER, J.D.R. (1971) *Black Child, White Child*, Cambridge, Mass., Harvard University Press.

PUSHKIN, K. (1967) *A Study of Ethnic Choices in the Play of Young Children in Three London Districts*, unpublished PhD thesis, Institute of Education, University of London.

RADKE, M., et al. (1949) 'Social perceptions and attitudes of children', *Genetical Psychology Monographs*, 40, pp. 327–447.

RADKE-YARROW, M., et al. (1952) 'The role of parents in the development of children's ethnic attitudes', *Child Development*, 23, pp. 13–53.

Ken Thomas

RATHS, L. (1943) 'Identifying the social acceptance of children', *Educational Research Bulletin*, 22.
RATHS, L. (1947) 'Evidence relating to the validity of the Ohio Social Acceptance Test', *Educational Research Bulletin*, 26, pp. 141–6.
RATHS, L. and SCHWEIKART, E.F. (1946) 'Social acceptance within interracial school groups', *Educational Research Bulletin*, 25, pp. 85–90.
RICHARDSON, S. and GREEN, A. (1971) 'When is black beautiful? Coloured and white children's reactions to skin colour', *British Journal of Educational Psychology*, 9.
ROBERTSON, T.S. and KAWWA, T. (1971) 'Ethnic relations between British and immigrant children', *Educational Research*, 13, 3.
ROWLEY, K.G. (1967) 'Social relations between British and immigrant children', *Educational Research*, 10, 2, pp. 145–9.
RUSHTON, J. (1967) 'A sociometric study of some immigrant children in Manchester schools', *Durham Research Review*, 19, 5, pp. 189–92.
ST. JOHN, N. and LEWIS, R.G. (1975) 'Race and the social structure of the elementary school classroom', *Sociology of Education*, 48, pp. 346–68.
SEGALL, M.H., *et al.* (1966) *The Influence of Culture on Visual Perception*, Indianapolis, Bobbs-Merrill.
SHAW, M.E. (1973) 'Changes in sociometric choices following forced integration of an elementary school', *Journal of Social Issues*, 29, 4, pp. 143–57.
SINGLETON, L.C. and ASHER, S.R. (1977) *A Developmental Study of Sociometric Choices in Integrated Classrooms*, paper read to the American Psychological Association, San Francisco, August 1977.
SINGLETON, L.C., *et al.* (1976) 'Sociometric ratings and social interaction among third grade children in an integrated school district', *Journal of Classroom Interaction*, 12, 1, pp. 71–82.
SPRINGER, D. (1950) 'Awareness of racial differences by pre-school children in Hawaii', *General Psychology Monographs*, 41, pp. 215–70.
STEVENSON, H.W. and STEWART, H.C. (1958) 'A developmental study of racial awareness in young children', *Child Development*, 29, pp. 399–409.
SUMMERS, G.F. and HAMMOND, A.D. (1966) 'Effect of racial characteristics of investigator on self enumerated responses to a Negro prejudice scale', *Social Forces*, 44, pp. 515–18.
TAJFEL, H., *et al.* (1970) 'The development of children's preferences for their country: A cross national study', *International Journal of Psychology*, 5, 4, pp. 245–53.
THOMAS, K.C. (1975) 'Race in the curriculum', *The New Era*, 56, 7, pp. 10–13.
THOMAS, K.C. (1981) *A Study of Stereotypes, Peer-Group Friendship Patterns and Attitudes in a Multi-Racial School*, unpublished PhD thesis, School of Education, University of Nottingham.
THOMAS, K.C. (1982) 'Race of tester effects on sociometric friendship ratings', *Educational Studies*, 8, 2, pp. 103–11.
TRENT, R.D. (1954) 'The colour of investigator as a variable in experimental research with Negro subjects', *Journal of Social Psychology*, 40, pp. 281–7.

TROYNA, B.S. (1978) 'Race and streaming: A case study', *Educational Review*, 30, 1, pp. 59–65.

VAN DEN BERGHE, P.L. (1968) *Race and Racism*, New York, John Wiley and Sons.

VAUGHAN, G.M. (1963) 'Concept formation and the development of ethnic awareness', *Journal of Genetical Psychology*, 103, pp. 119–30.

VAUGHAN, G.M. (1964a) 'Ethnic awareness in relation to minority group membership', *Journal of Genetic Psychology*, 105, pp. 119–30.

VAUGHAN, G.M. (1964b) 'The effects of the ethnic grouping of the experimenter upon children's responses to tests of an ethnic nature', *British Journal of Social and Clinical Psychology*, 3, pp. 66–70.

VAUGHAN, G.M. (1964c) 'The development of ethnic attitudes in New Zealand school-children', *General Psychology Monographs*, 70, pp. 135–75.

VAUGHAN, G.M. and THOMPSON, R.H.T. (1961) 'New Zealand children's attitudes towards Maoris', *Journal of Abnormal Social Psychology*, 62, pp. 701–4.

WILSON, W.C. (1963) 'Development of ethnic attitudes in adolescence', *Child Development*, 34, pp. 247–56.

Language Issues in School

Viv Edwards

This chapter offers a broad review of what constitutes a central feature of educational theory and practice in multicultural Britain, and argues that linguistic diversity represents a valuable classroom resource.

Standard English is the variety of English associated with the socially powerful. It owes its status to an historical accident rather than any inherent linguistic quality (Leith, 1983), and there is no reason why education should not be conducted in Geordie or Scouse or Highland Scots. But, while it is possible to argue from a purely linguistic standpoint that no language or dialect is superior to any other, the fact remains that standard English is the most prestigious form of English and that educational success and social mobility are dependent on the ability to use it.

The traditional response of the school to the linguistic diversity which has always existed has been to attempt to eradicate varieties other than the standard. In the first half of this century, the rationale for this approach was that only the standard could provide the necessary conceptual framework for learning and that other varieties were inadequate. The development of linguistics as a serious science pointed to flaws in such an argument, and more recently teachers have tended to justify their exclusive concentration on the standard in terms of helping their pupils to achieve educational success. Yet the fact remains that the vast majority of the British population does not speak standard English either on entering school at the age of 5, or on leaving at the age of 16.

Language has thus been the focus of educational debate for a very long time. This debate gained considerably in momentum and broadened in scope during the 1960s when large numbers of children arrived from the New Commonwealth speaking a wide range of languages and overseas dialects of English. There has been a growing feeling that 'hospitality to diversity' is a more acceptable approach than one which criticizes and rejects the language which children bring with them to school (see DES, 1975; DES (Rampton) 1981; Levine, 1982), and an impressive number of initiatives which attempt to treat linguistic diversity as a classroom resource rather than a problem are being developed (see Edwards, 1983 for an overview of this area).

Linguistic Diversity and Bilingual Pupils

As somebody born and brought up in Wales, I consider myself first Welsh and next British, and have always objected when non-Britishers use 'English' as a cover-all term in preference to 'British'. It is important that such a personal statement should not be dismissed as nationalistic paranoia, since it both highlights and challenges certain widely accepted assumptions. On the one hand, the terminology employed by non-Britons underlines the cultural and linguistic dominance of the English in the British Isles. On the other hand, the fact that I and many others have a strong sense of ethnic minority membership undermines the notion of monolingualism and mono-culturalism which permeates most British institutions, including education.

It would be wrong to restrict the dicussion of diversity in Britain to the Celtic-speaking fringes. Yiddish, Italian and Greek communities were well established in Britain before the Second World War, and the economic expansion of the post-war years attracted many other migrants, especially those from the New Commonwealth. The extent of linguistic diversity today is shown clearly in the Rosen and Burgess (1980) survey of London schools which established that some fifty-five different world languages were spoken by children in their sample. Linguistic homogeneity can thus be shown to be a total myth both today and in the past.

The arrival of large numbers of non-English speaking children in British schools during the 1960s forced people to think in new and interesting ways about issues which had long been present. The overriding concern of the early years of migration was the teaching of English. This proceeded in an atmosphere of 'muddling through'. There were very few teachers trained in this field and a total absence of suitable materials. Local authority autonomy meant that the nature and extent of provision varied enormously, there was little sharing of information and resources, and advice from central government was often slow, contradictory or non-existent (Edwards, 1983). The emphasis throughout this period was on the teaching of English by the 'direct method', and the various mother tongues of the children concerned were not considered to have any part to play in this process.

In more recent years, this approach to the teaching of English has received a good deal of criticism (Rampton, 1982). It has been argued, for instance, that it is harmful to children's self-esteem to find their language totally excluded from the school. Certainly, reports of teachers chiding pupils for the use of their mother tongue during playtime (Mercer, 1982), or of headteachers dismissing the teaching of Gujarati in terms of not wanting to start 'that caper' (Townsend, 1971) have done little to enhance the status of minority languages as legitimate vehicles of culture in their own right. Bitter complaints from the minority communities themselves of break-downs in communication between parents and children who cannot or will not use the mother tongue (Brown, 1979) point clearly to the tensions which such attitudes help to generate.

The burgeoning of community schools teaching the various mother tongues outside school hours has been one practical response to the very real frustrations created by an Anglocentric education system (Khan, 1980). It has, however, raised a number of important questions. For instance, opinion varies as to whether such provision should be the responsibility of the local authority or the minority community (Mercer, *op. cit.*). Although there is room for a wide range of responses, it would seem that such a large and important task can only be successfully undertaken with LEA assistance. But should such teaching take place inside or outside the normal curriculum? If it is accepted as part of the curriculum, it is obviously important to avoid timetable clashes with important subject options.

The strength of the mother tongue teaching lobby has been greatly advanced by arguments from other quarters. The late 1970s witnessed the formulation of policy within the European Economic Community concerning the language and education of the children of migrant workers. Member states are currently charged to promote mother tongue teaching 'in accordance with their national circum-stances and legal systems' (Council of Europe, 1977) and, although the British government has given very low priority to this area (Bellin, 1980), official attitudes towards mother tongue teaching certainly cannot be described as hostile.

Nonetheless, the mother tongue issue remains controversial. The prevailing wisdom within the teaching profession has long been that bilingualism is only desirable if the second language spoken is a high status Western European language such as French, German or Spanish, and the introduction of more exotic languages such as Urdu or Gujarati still meets with a good deal of resistance. The process of attitude change is inevitably slow. It should also be remembered that mother tongue teaching can be commended from a number of very different perspectives. It can be espoused as a cause just as enthusiastically by those of a radical persuasion who want members of ethnic minority communities to be able to compete on equal terms, as by racists who advocate the repatriation of migrants and their children. Within the radical camp there are also those who argue that mother tongue teaching will operate more effectively as an agent of social control than as a means of promoting cultural diversity (Brook, 1980). This is a matter which therefore demands careful thought and planning, and it is encouraging to note that many local authorities and teachers organizations such as the National Association for Multiracial Education and the National Association for the Teaching of English have produced detailed policy statements on the subject.

Linguistic Diversity and Dialect Speakers

It would be quite wrong to restrict discussion of linguistic diversity to bilingual pupils. The Rosen and Burgess (1980) survey of London schools revealed that many overseas varieties of English were spoken by children in their sample, especially Caribbean Creoles. Nor should we forget the considerable range of British dialects. It is an often overlooked fact that the vast majority of British people speak a non-standard dialect of English. The influx of bilingual pupils into British schools which resulted from post-war migration has forced a realization of the importance of the first language in identity, conceptual development and success in learning. Although the differences involved are very much smaller for dialect speakers than for bilingual pupils, the issues are substantially the same. It would clearly be illogical to recognize the importance of the language of the home for one group of children while ignoring it in the case of the other group.

Because the British education system is predicated upon the use of standard English, other dialects are at best overlooked and at worst heavily stigmatized. Since standard English is so closely associated with educational success and social mobility, resistance towards using it on the part of non-standard speakers might seem, at first sight, unduly perverse. However, attitudes towards language are complex. Although the prestige of standard English is universally recognized, standard speakers are often felt by dialect speakers to be prissy and even effeminate, while dialect speakers themselves are associated with trustworthiness and sincerity (Giles and Powesland, 1975). In the light of social forces such as these, most dialect speakers find the option of changing their speech patterns totally unacceptable. Faced with an education system which criticizes, rejects or ignores the language which they bring with them to school, they can respond by conforming to the norms of the school, or by withdrawal or defiance. The vast majority choose one of the last two of these courses. The attempt to impose monolingual, monocultural norms on children who speak non-standard dialects can thus be seen to be as counter-productive as the traditional response to bilingualism in schools.

The last twenty years have thus seen a marked shift in the direction of hospitality to diversity (Levine, 1982). Given the strength of feeling generated in any discussion of language in education, such developments have inevitably given rise to some controversy, and there are many dissenting voices among teachers and academics alike (see, for example, Honey, 1983). However, fears relating to the introduction of other languages and dialects into the classroom can be shown to be completely misplaced. By examining below three curriculum areas — talk, reading and writing — I will argue that the importance of language differences in education has been exaggerated, and that prescriptive attitudes to language on the part of teachers are a far more potent force in educational failure than the differences themselves.

Diversity and Talk

There is a widespread assumption that the only language suitable for educational purposes is standard English, and that the languages and dialects which children speak at home and in the community have no place in the classroom. Such a narrow approach fails to recognize the considerable linguistic resources which exist within every school. Rejection of the children's language is unlikely to enhance feelings of self-worth, essential for educational success. Acceptance of languages and dialects other than the standard, in contrast, indicates respect for the people who use them, and is far more likely to contribute to successful learning than criticism and rejection.

Traditionally, the curriculum has concentrated on the '3Rs' and children's talk was seen as a disruptive force rather than as a tool for learning. This is reflected to some extent in the way in which teachers monopolize the talk in many classes. Wood *et al.* (1980) demonstrate how adults dominate conversation, giving children little opportunity to think and answer, in nursery and playgroup settings. At the other end of the educational scale Stubbs (1976) draws our attention to the pattern of 'chalk and talk' lessons in which the teacher controls the direction of the lesson, placing children in a passive role in which they rarely initiate discussion and give short answers to well-defined questions.

However, there are alternative approaches to learning in which the pupil takes a more active role. When teachers do not bombard children with questions, allowing them to initiate exchanges and question the interpretation of what has been said, it is possible to achieve in a classroom setting something which approximates much more closely to what we would normally understand as discussion. We have only begun to understand the potential of discussion as an educational tool in recent years. The work of Barnes (1976) and Rosen and Rosen (1973), for instance, has argued persuasively that we learn more from talking than from listening. Discussion can also be seen to allow children practice in certain linguistic and conceptual skills; it also teaches social skills in children's relationships with each other (Richardson, 1982).

If a primary aim is to promote understanding through discussion, it is only reasonable that children should use the form of language they feel most comfortable with. The teacher who intervenes with ' "I didn't do it", John, not "I never done it" ' when a point has been well argued, will either be ignored or have a dampening effect upon the discussion. The principle of allowing discussion in the language children find comfortable obviously poses certain problems in the case of bilingual pupils who cannot argue a case in Punjabi or Turkish to a mixed audience. However, as Richardson (*op. cit.*) points out, there will be some occasions when it is both possible and desirable for children belonging to the same cultural or ethnic group to work together, in which case it would be natural for them to use their own first language where this is not English.

The promotion of talk in the classroom has particular advantages for the second language learner. When learning another language we approximate to the target language in a series of steps. 'Correction' by a teacher can be as ineffective and unwelcome in the case of the child learning English who urgently wishes to communicate a piece of information as it is in young children learning their first language. It is important, therefore, that second language learners should have access to as wide as possible a range of language — and not just the 'managerial' talk of the teacher — which will allow them to form hypotheses about words and structures. They must also have realistic opportunities to communicate with teachers and peers so as to test the validity of the rule systems they are developing.

Language has a central role in communication and learning, but it would be a serious omission to fail to discuss its play functions. Put starkly, we enjoy language and it is possible to capitalize on this enjoyment to motivate reading and writing, as well as other aspects of learning. The range of activities which draws upon the 'fun functions' of talk is virtually unlimited. The lore and language of school children, for instance, has been well documented by commentators such as the Opies. Skipping rhymes, playground rhymes, taunts and jokes can be tape-recorded, transcribed and illustrated. Comparison can be made between versions from different countries or different parts of the country, from parents and grandparents. Songs of insult from Greek Cypriot or Northern Indian weddings or the taunts of West Indian 'rhyming' (Edwards, 1983) add an interesting new dimension to known British practices.

Story telling is another valuable activity. Many ethnic minority children are privy to a tradition in which story telling is a highly prized and well-developed family and community activity. Although generally underexploited in British schools, it is possible to generate the same enthusiasm in children of all ages who have usually regarded stories as inextricably linked with the written rather than the spoken word (Rosen, 1982). Story telling may also be usefully encouraged in pupils with learning difficulties, since we tend to forget that even though such children may find the task of transcription frustrating or beyond their reach, they may nonetheless have a story to tell. Role play and drama also capitalize on children's enjoyment of language, and often allow them to demonstrate a surprising range of language and sensitivity to situation. Games and music can be used to similar effect.

The advantages of drawing on children's existing skills are two-fold. First, the children themselves are likely to grow in self-esteem and confidence from the feeling that their language and culture are valued and recognized by the school. Second, teachers are prodded from a preoccupation with what their pupils lack (i.e. a mastery of standard English) into an appreciation of skills seldom exercised in the classroom. Such an appreciation is likely to enhance teachers' awareness and expectations of children's potential for learning.

Diversity and Reading

Reading is seldom singled out as a learning activity which requires special strategies for the teacher in the multilingual classroom. It is certainly true that all children, irrespective of their linguistic background, are faced with similar problems and challenges at all stages of reading development. The teacher response to reading strategies, however, is of critical importance, and often difficulties which confront children reading in a language or dialect other than their own owe more to inappropriate teacher intervention than to actual differences in language background.

In order to make sense of what they read, children draw on graphic, syntactic and semantic information, and insert or omit words in a way which demonstrates that they are internalizing the text and re-encoding it in their own language. Thus, the child who reads: 'John put *his* books on the table' for 'John put *their* books on the table' has chosen *his* not because of any graphic similarity with *their* but because both words can fill the same grammatical slot in the sentence. An analysis of children's oral reading reveals many similar 'errors' — or, at most writers now call them (e.g., Smith, 1978; Gollasch, 1981), 'miscues' — which suggest that the reading process is something far more complex than a mere decoding operation. This view of reading has far-reaching implications for the teacher. For instance, a problem-solving approach, requiring children to use all the information at their disposal to arrive at an unknown word, is likely to be more appropriate than one which aims to develop purely mechanical decoding skills. A teacher who intervenes in the middle of children's reading may therefore be hindering the development of such problem-solving strategies, and may also detract from their pleasure in books by suggesting that the main object of the exercise is to foster perfectionist skills.

This important change in approach to the teaching of reading clearly has ramifications for children from all language backgrounds. The case of dialect speakers, however, deserves special attention. Difficulties caused by differences between the dialect of the reader and the dialect of the text have probably been overemphasized in recent years, and consideration of this area has distracted attention from the more pertinent question of the effect which teacher attitudes towards dialect differences may be having on children's reading performance. When we listen to the oral reading of children from many different language backgrounds, the tendency to translate a standard text into their own dialect soon becomes apparent. Thus a West Indian child might read: 'The *boy walk* down the street' for

'The *boys walked* down the street'. British working-class children from many parts of the country might read: 'He *come* home early in the morning' for 'He *came* home early in the morning' or 'We *was* talking when the teacher walked in' for 'We *were* talking when the teacher walked in.' Dialect-based miscues of this kind should not give rise to concern. The child is making use of existing knowledge to predict what comes next, clearly understands the text, and so is demonstrating very healthy reading strategies. The teacher who unnecessarily decides to 'correct' dialect features risks creating the impression that the main object of reading is to achieve word-for-word accuracy, and is more likely to produce a child who barks at print than one who reads for meaning.

The difficulties of bilingual pupils learning to read appear at first glance to be considerably more intractable than those which face dialect speakers. For instance, it would seem largely a matter of common sense that children find it easier to learn to read in their mother tongue than in a second language. However, research has shown the question to be a good deal more complex (Ramos *et al.*, 1967; Cohen *et al.*, 1973; Engles, 1975). The bilinguals who under-perform in reading and other aspects of education tend to belong to immigrant or ethnic minority groups who are in the process of being assimilated by the dominant majority, and not those who belong to majority language groups, irrespective of the medium of instruction. Thus in Britain, Punjabi-speaking children who learn to read in English tend to underperform, while English-speaking children who receive a Welsh medium education have a record of high achievement. By the same token, in a North American context, native Indian and Chicano children underperform, while Anglophone Canadians do equally well whether they are educated in English or French.

The actual reading behaviour of bilingual children has received very little attention in the literature. The fullest account of this area is probably contained in Goodman *et al.* (1979) who suggest that second language learners show three main kinds of behaviour:

1 noticeable but superficial differences in which case the process can still be relatively efficient and effective;
2 limitations in the ability of readers to express what they have understood in English;
3 some disruption to comprehension which may be minor or severe.

The first two patterns possibly give rise to more teacher concern than is necessary. For instance, the child who reads: 'Usually John *catch* the bus to school, but yesterday he *walk*' for 'Usually John *catches* the bus to school, but yesterday he *walked*' does not change the meaning of the passage in any way. Similarly, because our productive control of language often lags behind our receptive competence, children's difficulty in answering questions on a text, or retelling the story, may create the impression that their understanding of what they have read is far more limited than is actually the case.

Teachers can be forgiven for feeling disheartened at what may at first appear to be a bewildering range of needs in pupils from different language backgrounds who are learning to read. It should be remembered, however, that strategies such as not interrupting unnecessarily in the reading process, discussing the text, and working with material that interests the children (Edwards, 1983) which will help bilingual pupils to understand what they are reading, also promote the problem-solving approach which we have already discussed in relation to standard English and dialect-speaking children.

Diversity and Writing

Because standard English is so very closely linked with the written language, any deviation in children's writing inevitably attracts a great deal of attention. It is possible to argue, however, that non-standard and non-native forms in the writing of dialect-speaking and bilingual pupils give rise to a disproportionate amount of teacher concern, and detract from the most important pedagogic aim, *viz.* that of producing confident and competent writers.

Learning to write, like learning to read, presents similar problems for all children, regardless of language background. Like all learning processes it involves taking risks and making mistakes, and teacher attitudes towards these mistakes can be very important. For instance, it is invariably more instructive for all concerned when the teacher attempts to understand why a child has made a mistake, rather than simply marking it wrong. In the same way as the analysis of reading miscues reveals a great deal about the various strategies which are called into play when children learn to read, close scrutiny of writing errors offers many insights into how children learn to write. There is often evidence of the ability to recognize pattern. The child who writes *manchen* for *mansion* or *practersine* for *practising* is conforming to well-established written conventions, although they may not be the accepted conventions in these particular cases.

The language of writing differs in a number of respects from the spoken language. Because it can be read and reread, it is less redundant and repetitious; it is also organized in sentences, whereas speech is characterized for the most part by complexes of clauses (Kress, 1982). All children are therefore faced with the task of learning the organization, conventions and special structures associated with writing. Children for whom standard English is a second language or dialect necessarily face additional difficulties, but it is important to see these difficulties in perspective.

It would seem that the degree of difficulty posed by actual language differences has sometimes been exaggerated. Richmond (1979) shows in an analysis of samples of writing by a second generation Jamaican girl that 'errors, miscues and confusions' associated with technical aspects of writing and, in particular, spelling and punctuation, outnumber dialect features by something in the region of 4 to 1. Edwards (1983), in a similar analysis of writing by a British dialect speaker, shows that technical mistakes outnumber dialect features by 10 to 1. Difficulties of transcription clearly constitute a far greater problem for children than the intrusion of dialect features. Moreover, the conventions of transcription do not favour any specific social or ethnic group. Whereas children may well interpret teacher exhortations to avoid 'double negatives' as an attack on them and the way they speak, explanations concerning the placement of full stops and capital letters are socially neutral.

Detailed analysis of bilingual children's writing also pays dividends to the extent that it is possible to detect patterns which give likely indications of the best teacher response. Do children regularly make mistakes with a given feature such as past tenses or possessive *s*, or do they use the accepted form variably? If children make a mistake consistently, it would be appropriate to draw their attention to the feature in question and provide practice in using it correctly. If, however, a form is used incorrectly only on some occasions, this might well be the kind of slip of the pen which even native children make, and should not give rise to concern. Thus, in some cases, immediate attention will be required, while in others it will be best not to intervene but to monitor the child's progress over a period of time. In all cases, a *global* appreciation of the child's weaknesses and strengths (Studdert and Wiles, 1982) highlighting areas of weakness rather than isolating particular instances (which may or may not point to more widespread difficulties) will be most helpful. It would be totally impractical to suggest that teachers should closely analyze every piece of writing which a child produces; but the monitoring of selected work at regular intervals will help the teacher to identify patterns which indicate why a child is making mistakes, and whether specific intervention is necessary.

Many teachers react with horror to the suggestion that certain dialect features and second language learning errors should not be drawn to children's attention, equating such an approach with falling standards and holding children back. However, such a position is quite untenable. Teachers simply do not have the time to correct every departure from standard English; they are also very aware of the demoralizing effect on children of receiving a piece of work covered in red correction marks. In practice they tend to engage in 'selective marking' (Edwards, 1983) which is often extremely inconsistent. Cheshire (1982), for instance, cites the example of a teacher who, in the same short passage of writing, overlooks two instances of non-standard *was* for *were*, puts a cross above the third, and underlines the fourth and fifth, writing in *were* above them. Such an approach is hardly likely to convey to the child that in standard English plural subjects always require the *were* form. Marking must of necessity be selective, but it need not be haphazard. Careful monitoring of children's writing will help the teacher identify the most urgent and achievable teaching targets, and departures from standard English will often come very low on the list of priorities.

The aim of producing children who can write standard English is seen by many as incompatible with allowing any other kind of writing in the classroom. Yet it is vitally important that writing should be both a meaningful and interesting experience for children (Smith, 1982), and it may well be more appropriate or natural for children who want to write about a particular situation or theme to use the language normally associated with it. This kind of experience encourages an awareness in children of the appropriateness of different language varieties for different situations, and does not in any way detract from the educational goal of producing children who are literate in standard English. Such a goal depends on children who have a well-developed sense of themselves as writers. Any attempt to draw upon existing linguistic skills is likely to contribute to this sense; devaluing or ignoring these skills is likely to achieve the opposite effect.

Conclusion

It is very important that linguistic diversity should be looked upon as a classroom resource rather than a problem. Traditionally, standard

English has been considered the only acceptable variety in the classroom and other languages and dialects have been relegated to the playground and the street. The strict insistence on standard English, however, is both impractical and counterproductive. For instance, strategies involved in learning to read and write are the same for all children, and do not vary with language background. The teacher who 'corrects' departures from the standard in oral reading therefore detracts from the problem-solving approach necessary for fluent reading, and is likely to foster a child who strives for word-for-word accuracy rather than understanding. Similarly, an insistence on standard forms in writing detracts from the far more pressing problems of transcription, and does nothing to encourage children's sense of themselves as writers. Acceptance of other language varieties in the classroom can thus be seen as a means of developing awareness of which forms are appropriate in which situations, and can help to extend rather than limit children's linguistic repertoires. Certainly, tolerance of other languages and dialects in education is not in any way incompatible with fostering the use of standard English. For, whereas criticism and rejection of other languages and dialects is likely to provoke either hostility to attempts to impose the standard, or withdrawal, acceptance and recognition of children's language and culture are likely to enhance their confidence and standing among their peers, and represent a far healthier starting point for successful learning.

References

BARNES, D. (1976) *From Communication to Curriculum*, Harmondsworth, Penguin.

BELLIN, W. (1980) 'The EEC Directive on the Education of the Children of Migrant Workers: A comparison of the Commission's proposed directive and the Council directive together with a parallel text', *Polyglot*, 2, Fiche 2.

BROOK, M. (1980) 'The "mother tongue" issue in Britain: cultural diversity or control?', *British Journal of Sociology of Education*, 1, 3, pp. 237–57.

CHESHIRE, J. (1982) 'Dialect features and linguistic conflict in School' *Educational Review*, 34, 1, pp. 53–67.

COHEN, A. *et al.* (1973) 'The Culver City Spanish Immersion Program: End of Year #1 and Year #2', Mimeo, Department of English, University of California at Los Angeles.

COUNCIL OF EUROPE (1977) *Council Directive on the Education of the Children of Migrant Workers*, 77/48b/EEC, 25 July.

DES (1975) *A Language for Life*, ('Bullock Report'), London, HMSO.

DES (1981) *West Indian Children in Our Schools*, Interim Report of the Committee of Inquiry into the Education of Children from Ethnic Minority Groups ('Rampton Report'), London, HMSO.

EDWARDS, V. (1983) *Language in Multicultural Classrooms*, London, Batsford Academic.

ENGLES, D. (1975) *The Use of Vernacular Languages in Education*, Arlington, Va., Center for Applied Linguistics.

GILES, H. and POWESLAND, P. (1975) *Speech Style and Social Evaluation*, London and New York, Academic Press.

GOLLASCH, F. (1981) *The Language and Literacy: The Selected Writings of Kenneth S. Goodman*, Vol. 1: Process, Theory, Research. London, Routledge and Kegan Paul.

GOODMAN, K. *et al.* (1979) *Reading in the Bilingual Classroom: Literacy and Biliteracy*, Rosslyn, Va., National Clearinghouse for Bilingual Education.

HONEY, J. (1983) *The Language Trap: Race, Class and the Standard English Issue in British Schools*, Kenton, Middlesex, National Council for Educational Standards.

KAHN, V. (1980) 'The "mother-tongue" of linguistic minorities in multicultural England', *Journal of Multilingual and Multicultural Development*, 1, 1, pp. 71–88.

KRESS, G. (1982) *Learning to Write*, London, Routledge and Kegan Paul.

LEITH, D. (1983) *A Social History of English*, London, Routledge and Kegan Paul.

LEVINE, J. (1982) 'Developing pedagogies for multilingual classes', *English in Education*, 15, 3, pp. 25–33.

MERCER, L. (1981) 'Ethnicity and the supplementary school', in MERCER, N. (Ed.), *Language in School and Community*, London, Edward Arnold, pp. 147–60.

OPIE, I. and OPIE, P. (1977) *The Lore and Language of Schoolchildren*, St Albans, Paladin.

RAMOS, M. *et al.* (1967) *The Determination and Implementation of Language Policy*, Quezon City, Pheonix Press.

RAMPTON, M.B. (1982) *The English of UK Ethnic Minority School Children of South Asian Extraction*, MA dissertation, University of London Institute of Education.

RICHARDSON, R. (1982) 'Talking about equality: The use and importance of discussion in multi-cultural education', *Cambridge Journal of Education*, 12, 2, pp. 101–14.

RICHMOND, J. (1979) 'Dialect features in mainstream school writing', *New Approaches to Multiracial Education*, 8, 1, pp. 9–15.

ROSEN, M. (1982) 'Three papers: Writers in Inner City Residence; In Their Own Voice; Our Culture — a Definition by Description of its Parts,' in Talk Workshop Group (1982), *Becoming Our Own Experts: The Vauxhall Papers*, pp. 378–91.

ROSEN, H. and BURGESS, T. (1980) *Language and Dialects of London School Children*, London, Ward Lock Educational.

ROSEN, C. and ROSEN, H. (1973) *The Language of Primary School Children*, Harmondsworth, Penguin.

SMITH, F. (1978) *Reading*, Cambridge, Cambridge University Press.

SMITH, F. (1982) *Writing and the Writer*, London, Heinemann Educational.

STUBBS, M. (1976) *Language, Schools and Classrooms*, London, Methuen.

STUDDERT, J. and WILES, S. (1982) 'Children's writing in the multilingual classroom', *Centre for Urban Educational Studies Occasional Paper*, Spring.

TOWNSEND, H.E.R. (1971) *Immigrants in England: The LEA Response*, Windsor, National Foundation for Educational Research.

WOOD, D. *et al.* (1980) *Working with Under Fives*, London, Grant McIntyre.

Bilingualism and Mother Tongue Teaching in England*

The Linguistic Minorities Project

In this chapter, some of the broader, societal aspects of language diversity are discussed and some first research findings are reported by a leading British research unit in the field.

There are many bilingual adults in England who altered their patterns of language use when they migrated from their homelands. In the future, however, there will be increasing numbers of British-born bilinguals who learn their 'mother tongue' from their parents, relatives and friends and in local community-based activities. The environmental support these young people experience for their other-than-English language depends, of course, on how many people use these languages around them, who these people are, and what purposes the languages serve.

The opportunities bilingual adults have to use their other-than-English language depend on their patterns of social interaction, which are influenced in large measure by the local labour market. Their British-born bilingual children grow up with two or more languages,

* This chapter is based on work in progress which is to be published in *The Other Languages of England* by Routledge and Kegan Paul in 1984. Permission for the use of these extracts is gratefully acknowledged. The authors are Marilyn Martin-Jones, Anna Morawska, Euan Reid, Verity Saifullah Khan, and Greg Smith (from the DES-funded Linguistic Minorities Project); and Xavier Couillaud (from the EEC-funded Language Information Network Coordination Project, which is attached to LMP). The authors wish to acknowledge the valuable work of Michael Morawski, Judy Tasker, Carrie Harvey and Christine Dean, Jenny Norvick, Delores Reviere and Mee-Lian Yong.

often using them in a variety of contexts. These languages are learnt informally at first, but from the age of 5 onwards the language socialization of the home, kin, the peer group and the local community interact with the more formal processes of language learning offered by the local state school, and in some cases local community-run teaching provision.

If we are to understand the impact of language learning on the overall educational development of pupils in our schools, we need to understand these different processes and how they influence the different language varieties of a child's linguistic repertoire. Most important of all, we need to analyze how the learning of the two or three languages is related in different contexts and over time. For example, increasing numbers of pupils attend classes in their mother tongue or first language, organized outside the regular state school system. In some of these classes English is rarely used; in others, it is the medium of instruction for teaching the so-called 'mother tongue'.

Knowledge of the distribution and sociolinguistic characteristics of different linguistic minorities helps also to inform the debate about which minority languages could be taught in the state school system, and which varieties are most appropriate for different purposes (NCLE, 1983). It is dangerous, however, to look at this question of 'mother tongue' teaching in isolation. An understanding of the educational implications of bilingualism ought to involve studies of language use beyond the school and among the adult population, since the impact of language policies at school can only be understood in the context of language use in the full range of the pupils' social activities. Patterns of language use in the family and in the locality are bound to influence the degree of mother tongue retention in future school populations. We need to know not only when and where minority languages are being used, but how important they are to the speakers concerned. Do they really have many opportunities to use their other than English languages? What kind of formal mother tongue teaching is arranged by the local population? Do many parents know about the possibility of introducing mother tongue teaching in the state school system, and do they support the idea? Do their children feel confident enough to talk about or use their mother tongue on the premises of their local state school? What proportion of them is attending local community-run language classes in the evenings or at weekends?

Both bidialectal and bilingual speakers adapt their language use according to context and according to whom they are with. In the ways in which they draw on their linguistic repertoire they convey different aspects of their social identity. In the formal school situation, many of these choices of language use are made for pupils. Although there is increasing agreement among educationalists that teachers should make use of the full range of the cultural and linguistic resources their pupils bring to school, if this is not encouraged the pupils no longer offer all of these resources. They are quick to interpret indirect messages about appropriateness and value. If other similar messages accumulate over time they may gradually lose their knowledge of these non-English linguistic 'resources'.

This personal loss is also a loss for our society which goes far beyond the educational advantages for the individual of being bilingual and the personal damage inflicted by denying children part of their potential development. The subordination of a language is a subtle means of dominating a people, and in the context of England it is another means of restricting the social and intellectual horizons of English monolinguals.

If bilingualism is seen to be a personal and societal resource and not only relevant for bilingual members of our society, it is the concern of all those who are interested in developing the social and economic resources of the country. These arguments need to be repeated alongside another fundamental perspective. Many people think that questions of mother tongue teaching or the future of linguistic minorities are new issues for England. But they are not new issues in many other parts of the world, and, more importantly for educationalists in England, the basic questions that are being asked are age-old questions about the educational development of children. Contemporary discussions about language across the curriculum, linguistic awareness, education for a multicultural society, etc. all refer ultimately to the same questions of ensuring that the children develop their full linguistic potential, and thereby extend their educational and social horizons.

Countering the generally held stereotypes which feed problematic assimilationist perspectives, and the view of bilingualism as somehow abnormal, is not an easy task. Nor is it easy to develop a research project in a situation where there is very little information, and often a variety of interests and conflicting definitions of what is happening. But, taking seriously the policy interests supporting our project, we designed a school-based survey, the Schools Language Survey (SLS), to find out about the range of linguistic diversity throughout an education authority. This survey was to be carried out in approximately six LEAs. We were insistent, however, that such a basic policy-related exercise should be supplemented by a more sociolinguistic research instrument, which allowed a sample of bilingual and monolingual school pupils to record their own perceptions and patterns of language use. This Secondary Pupils Survey (SPS) and the other two community-based surveys, the Mother Tongue Teaching Directory and the Adult Language Use Survey, were carried out only in a few areas of England, with the intention that the data from the different surveys would complement each other and create a background for more detailed case studies by researchers in the future.

The Main Linguistic Minorities in England

The first step toward an understanding of the sociolinguistic position of linguistic minorities in England is to look at the historical and political developments which have determined the relationship between the people who speak the minority languages and the dominant majority.

The majority of the linguistic minorities in England consist of people who arrived between 1940 and 1975 and their descendants. The populations and languages which arrived in England can be broadly typified along two intersecting dimensions, as well as along a time axis. First, linguistic minorities can be distinguished according to the motivation for the original migration and settlement. Some came primarily as political refugees, while others came primarily as migrant labour. The second dimension is place of origin, which can be broadly dichotomized between ex-colonial Third World countries and European countries. This dimension broadly corresponds to distinctions of 'race' and skin colour, which, during the period in question, have been the main feature of the political debate about immigration policy.

Schematically the main linguistic minority populations can be located as shown in Table 1. The Cypriot minorities are the most difficult to fit into this schema, since they originate from an ex-colony which is not generally regarded as a Third World country, and in the 1960s came as labour migrants. However, people arriving from Cyprus since the war of 1974 can be regarded as refugees. Also excluded from this schema are those who came as students, typically from Africa, Malaysia and Singapore.

The socio-historical background of each population is one major influence when the majority society makes its assessment of the status of these people and of their languages. The differential statuses of linguistic minorities reflect the importance of political relations (e.g.,

Table 1.   *Linguistic Minorities in England*

	Migrant Labour	Political Refugees
Ex-colonial origin	Bengali, Punjabi, Gujerati (1960–75) Hong Kong Chinese (West Indians)	East African Asians (1968–73) Vietnamese (1979–82)
	Turkish and Greek Cypriots	
European origin	Italians (1950 onwards) Portuguese, Spanish	Polish, Ukrainian and other East Europeans (1945–50)

'immigration' may be taken to mean 'race'), and the degree of perceived cultural distinctiveness.

Between 1945 and 1975 the largest labour migrations which developed around the economic needs of post-war England were fed by people from ex-colonies, who initially had legal rights of settlement and citizenship. As non-European and ex-subject peoples they were peceived to be of a far lower status than any European people. However, despite the relatively high status accorded to the Southern European languages such as Italian and Spanish, and changes in nationality and immigration law which have tended to favour citizens of European countries at the expense of citizens of the Commonwealth ones, their position as migrant workers means that bilingual pupils from these minorities are not perceived as a resource for the predominantly monolingual school. These Spanish-English or Italian-English speaking pupils are not seen in the same light as the privileged pupils at London lycées, but are perceived as economic migrants of lower socioeconomic background.

Each of the instruments designed by LMP had its own focus and methods. To a certain extent, this meant that our definitions of linguistic minorities in general and in particular needed to differ according to our purpose. This meant that the boundaries of the linguistic minorities were inevitably defined by different criteria and sometimes by different people. For example, in the Adult Language Use Survey the set of *potential* respondents was defined by the researchers, usually on the basis of 'ethnic' criteria such as family name or membership of a community organization; while the set of *actual* respondents was defined by negotiation between the interviewer and the person on the doorstep, in response to a preliminary discussion as to whether they spoke the language in question. In the Mother Tongue Teaching Directory Survey, the boundary of linguistic minorities was defined on the basis of which languages were taught by schools in the voluntary or statutory sector. For example, if a school taught Chinese to children from Hakka, Cantonese and Hokkien language backgrounds together, it had defined its linguistic minority as the broader category of 'Chinese'. In both school surveys the researchers only encountered the boundary problems after the data had been returned. The Schools Language Survey relied on teachers' perceptions (plus our notes and the pupils' answers) to define groups of pupils with the same or different languages. The Secondary Pupils Survey, on the other hand, gave pupils much more freedom to place themselves inside or outside one of the linguistic minorities, although their decision was obviously affected by the atmosphere of the classroom and the influence of teacher and peer group.

As there are some neighbourhoods in certain cities where 'linguistic minorities' or even a single 'linguistic minority' form a numerical majority of the local population, we should make it clear from the beginning that the term 'minority' when used in a quantitative sense is to be interpreted within the *national* context. Furthermore, our conception of linguistic minorities incorporates the dimension of relative powerlessness, which distinguishes subordinate minorities from the dominant majority in terms of their access to economic, political and cultural resources. The starting point for a definition of *linguistic* minority is that it is a category of people who share a language which is not the language of the dominant majority, i.e., a language other than English. This, of course, does not exclude the possibility that migrants already had some English when they first arrived in England. For example, many migrants from the Indian subcontinent had some knowledge of, or familiarity with, the English language since it plays an important role within India, Pakistan and Bangladesh today.

A definition based on 'sharing a language' is clearly a minimal one, and may include people who identify with a given language and/or the collectivity in which it is used, without themselves possessing a wide range of linguistic skills, or even regularly speaking or fully understanding the language. On the other hand, people may use the language in question fluently and often without necessarily identifying with the linguistic minority, and these would be included by the minimal definition. This definition is a social one, delimiting the set of people for whom a 'language' (in this sense a symbolic entity that they themselves define) has either affective or communicative significance. It is a definition which to a large extent must rely on subjective information provided by members of the minority in question, rather than on categories chosen by researchers on the basis of linguistic behaviour.

The Context of Three Cities

The three cities in which LMP carried out the majority of its work exemplify the situation of linguistic minorities throughout the country. There are common factors in the economic and social settings in Coventry, Bradford and London, yet there are also local differences which make each city unique for its mixture of languages, and for the housing, employment and educational resources available to the people living there.

The pattern of settlement of all the recent linguistic minorities has largely been determined at the regional level by employment opportunities. They have therefore been concentrated to a large extent in unskilled work in the heavy industrial sector in the West Midlands, in the declining textile industry in West Yorkshire and Lancashire, and in a range of industries in London and the South-East (notably the clothing trade in the East End in the case of Bengalis, the retail trade in small shops in the case of the Gujeratis, and in various industrial and service sectors for speakers of other languages). These patterns have been greatly influenced by structural changes in industry, and the pressures of local labour markets, coupled with institutionalized and overt discriminatory practices which have tended to exclude minorities from many of the better jobs. In most cases, the process of chain migration and the practice of recruitment by personal recommendation has increased the level of segregation on the shop floor.

However, the distribution of languages at the neighbourhood level within each city seems to be related much more closely to housing patterns. With certain exceptions, families of recent migrants are rarely to be found in the public sector of the housing market, but have become established as owner occupiers in the inner areas of cities where property is relatively cheap and close to major workplaces. The details of employment, housing and social situations of the different linguistic minorities of course vary from city to city, and some of the main demographic features are illustrated in Tables 2, 3 and 4.

Table 2. *Summary of Significant Demographic Features of the Main Linguistic Minorities in Coventry*

				Language				
	Chinese	Gujerati	Italian	Panjabi (G)*	Panjabi (U)*	Polish	Bengali	Ukrainian
Estimate of total population	300	4,500	600	15,000	2,000	1,500	600	300
Numbers of households with member interviewed	43	203	108	200	86	168	79	48
Number of people in the respondents' households	213	992	394	1,025	482	471	374	144
Percentage of people in respondents' households aged below 17	43	30	22	41	53	14	49	11
Percentage of households in owner occupation	61	91	96	98	94	92	75	88
Percentage of households in council housing	12	6	2	—	1	7	14	10
Percentage of males aged 17–65 at work outside home or in family business	72	74	82	78	73	80	72	78

Percentage of females aged 17–60 at work outside home or in family business	43	42	67	39	11	57	13	63
Percentage of people in respondents' households brought up overseas	56	56	49	45	41	54	51	60

Source: LMP Adult Language Use Survey.

Note: *Most families in England with origins in the Panjab, whether in Indian Panjab or Pakistani Panjab, and whether they are Muslim, Sikh or Hindu, use spoken forms of Panjabi which are mutually intelligible. However, in our Adult Survey, the Panjabi speakers were treated as two separate linguistic minorities, because of the different ways of writing their closely similar spoken varieties. We designated one 'Panjabi-Gurmukhi script', and the other 'Panjabi — Urdu script', abbreviated as Panjabi (G) and Panjabi (U) respectively.

Table 3. *Summary of Significant Demographic Features of the Main Linguistic Minorities in Bradford*

	Language			
	Chinese	Panjabi (G)*	Panjabi (U)*	Polish
Estimate of total population	250	6,000	37,000	2,000
Number of households with member interviewed	50	98	177	155
Number of people in respondents' households	244	529	1,033	449
Percentage of people in respondents' households aged below 17	51	42	50	14
Percentage of households in owner occupation	—	99	96	93
Percentage of households in council housing	28	—	1	6
Percentage of males aged 17–65 at work outside home or in family business	9	72	61	70
Percentage of females aged 17–60 at work outside home or in family business	9	42	1	61
Percentage of people in respondents' households brought up overseas	87	42	43	51

Source: LMP Adult Language Use Survey.
Note: * See footnote to Table 2.

Table 4. *Summary of Significant Demographic Features of the Main Linguistic Minorities in London*

	Chinese	Bengali	Gujerati	Language Greek	Turkish	Italian	Portuguese
Numbers of households with member interviewed	137	185	99	193	197	94	196
Number of people in the respondents' households	597	898	457	758	822	367	627
Percentage of people in respondents' households aged below 17	33	44	23	25	30	30	24
Percentage of households in owner occupation	37	22	77	86	84	62	10
Percentage of households in council housing	37	65	16	8	9	32	28
Percentage of males aged 17–65 at work outside home or in family business	60	82	77	76	76	87	94
Percentage of females aged 17–60 at work outside home or in family business	37	11	44	43	32	75	73
Percentage of people in respondents' households brought up overseas	58	53	70	52	48	42	69

Source: LMP Adult Language Use Survey.

There are many factors which speed up or slow down what is often believed to be an inevitable process of 'shift' from bilingualism to monolingualism in the dominant language in countries of immigration. 'Language shift' is the habitual use of one language being replaced by the habitual use of another. It is a reflection of power relations in a society, producing a redistribution of social and linguistic resources from generation to generation.

Factors affecting language maintenance may be fundamental external forces influencing the economic, political and social resources of a linguistic minority. They may also be factors emerging from *within* the minority, and within a situation of contact between cultures. This 'internal' response is often a reaction to outside pressure. Geographical concentration, time of migration, relationship to the local labour market, social mobility and degrees of social conflict and competition over scarce resources are only some of the factors which influence the process of language shift. There are also different kinds of majority and minority institutional support, such as radio and television programmes in minority languages, minority owned press, or community-run schools and churches. While we can describe the main social circumstances which encourage the maintenance of minority languages at local level (Linguistic Minorities Project, 1984; Community Languages and Education Project, 1984–85), it is hard to isolate specific sets of factors whose presence allows prediction.

Considering the wide range of factors influencing language maintenance and transmission from one generation to another, there will inevitably be very different situations within the same linguistic minority in different cities. Language shift, and assimilation to the dominant language and culture, may be an overall national trend, but this does not preclude the possibility of a more stable bilingualism in some local linguistic minorities.

There are two institutions which have a particularly important role in the transmission of minority language skills over time; these are the family and minority associations, and details of the language skills and language use of the linguistic minorities indicated in Tables 2–4 will be available shortly (Linguistic Minorities Project, 1984, and Community Languages and Education Project, 1984–85). It is only with knowledge of reported skills that we can begin to interpret patterns of language use. Some adults do not have the opportunity to use their minority language in certain spheres of social activity (e.g., work), or in certain relationships (e.g., with their children). Our data look at language use in the household, and in other spheres of social activity beyond the home and at work, taking into account the language skills and the patterns of language use of other people in the same setting.

The next section looks at one institution which has an important role in the transmission of language skills from one generation to another, namely, community language classes (or 'supplementary schools').

Mother Tongue Teaching Provision

Mother tongue schools and classes are important institutional bases for the maintenance and reproduction of language skills, as well as of ethnic or religious affiliation, but their function and efficacy is likely to change over time. Some schools have already consciously changed their objectives and the methods and content of teaching, for example, in response to the changes in the linguistic experience of their pupils. Others have changed in response to external events, such as the arrival of a new wave of migration from a different geographical area or political system, e.g., South Asians arriving from East Africa in the early 1970s, or Polish refugees arriving after December 1981. Developments in local and national ethnic relations have also influenced the involvement of LEA schools in the 'mother tongue' issue, and the relationship between LEA and community-run provision.

Affiliation to particular minority associations, contact with people from urban backgrounds, access to libraries, newspapers and films are likely to support or develop skills in the standard national language, rather than in the spoken vernaculars of most homes. Although there are great differences in the aims and origins of mother tongue classes in the various languages, one of their main common functions is the introduction of literacy. The relationship between oral/aural and literacy skills varies in different minorities and is especially complex in some multilingual populations, for whom the language of literacy is not that spoken at home. It is certainly important not to base all the arguments for supporting mother tongue teaching on an assumption that what is taught has a necessarily direct linguistic relationship to the child's first home language, but to place this mother tongue teaching in its social context. This wider context helps us appreciate the collective and symbolic value of the minority language. It is only when we know more about the social circumstances in which pupils live that we can appreciate the relationship of these pupils not only to their already acquired but also to the presently taught languages, which are all potentially spoken and written varieties within their linguistic repertories.

Although 'mother tongue' teaching has been in existence in England for a long time, few people beyond those immediately involved have known much about the various dimensions and sources of support for such teaching until very recently. This has meant that not only have many minority organizations been ignorant of mother tongue teaching initiatives among other minorities in their own area, but that they have often also been unaware of initiatives within their own population in other cities. In 1976 many LEA officers and local teachers either had no knowledge of the existence of mother tongue provision, or did not recognize that it was fundamental to the general educational development of their pupils (Khan, 1977, 1980). When minority organizations asked for financial support, or minority teachers working in the LEA schools introduced mother tongue lessons in school breaks or after school, they were often perceived by the educational authorities as exceptional cases and not as reflecting a more general need or trend.

Since 1979 there has been more public discussion about mother tongue teaching within the context of other educational developments. The greatest impetus to the debate has, however, been a result of the organized pressure and articulated demand coming from the minority groups themselves. This was given a considerable boost in 1976 by the Draft Directive on the Education of Migrant Workers' Children of the European Communities (European Communities 1977; Tosi, 1979). The initial almost total rejection of the principles it proposed by many LEAs and teachers' unions, without constructive discussion based on sound information, produced a reaction from a wide range of minority organizations. In the period 1976–78 there were the first formal links between the European and South Asian interests, in the setting up of the Coordinating Committee for Mother-Tongue Teaching (now the National Council for Mother-Tongue Teaching), and greater coordination between mainstream educational and community relations associations and minority organizations.

One way of briefly introducing the different relationships that mother tongue teaching organizations have with their local communities, and with their LEA schools, is to describe the typical forms of organization for the main groups of languages. First, there are the Eastern European languages such as Polish and Ukrainian which are the national languages of originally refugee populations which settled in Britain after the Second World War. Schools were usually set up by parents' groups, often under the auspices of the local church, e.g., for the Polish communities. In most cases no help was received from the LEAs, although it is clear that in certain towns assistance was sought. These populations frequently provide well-organized locally-run provision, supported in some of the populations by central educational bodies such as the Polish Macierz Szkolna.

The second major group of languages includes Bengali, Gujerati, Hindi, Panjabi and Urdu, the languages of those more recent South Asian migrants from the Indian subcontinent, and South Asians from East Africa. After an initial period of settling down, most of these populations started teaching the national or regional language of the place of origin, along with languages for religious purposes. In many cases, this provision was developed by, and sometimes in conjunction with, those running religious institutions, and sometimes the inability to keep up with the increasing demand for teaching resulted in assistance being sought and occasionally granted by LEAs.

The third major category of languages includes Italian, Spanish, Portuguese, Greek and Turkish, i.e., Southern European languages belonging, in some cases, to people who have migrant worker status in British society (such as Italian and Greek spoken by nationals of EEC Member States). Whereas most of the previous populations mentioned have had little 'official' support from their countries of origin, most of the Southern European communities have government support in the provision of teachers or their salaries, materials and funds for accommodation and other expenses. In some cases, there is also support from the churches or local parents' associations. However, there are some cases which do not easily fit these general categories, such as the Chinese schools run under a variety of auspices including local parents' associations, students, churches and missions.

The data presented in Table 5 derive from an analysis of the Stage I questionnaire of the Mother Tongue Teaching Directory Survey. This survey instrument was developed in collaboration with the National Council for Mother Tongue Teaching. Despite the problems of devising and administering the survey, these findings provide a good indication of the scope and coverage of mother tongue schools and classes in the three cities where we worked, e.g., the number of linguistic minorities involved, the number and age of pupils, the organizational and financial arrangements.

The classes in the different language groups were founded in different periods, relating of course to the settlements of the various populations. After the earliest class we have reference to (the Hebrew

Table 5. Material Support from LEAs for Mother Tongue Classes

Language	Coventry 1981			Bradford 1981			Haringey 1982		
	A	B	C	A	B	C	A	B	C
Arabic	—	—	—	1	1	10	0	0	1
Bengali	—	—	—	0	2	0	0	3	0
Chinese	0	0	3	0	0	5	0	0	11
Greek	0	3	0	0	0	3	12	4	74
Gujerati	4	14	2	1	0	8	0	0	1
Hebrew	—	—	—	—	—	—	0	0	7
Hindi	5	0	1	0	1	2	0	0	2
Irish Gaelic	—	—	—	—	—	—	1	0	0
Italian	2	0	7	0	18	0	0	0	12
Latvian	—	—	—	0	0	2	—	—	—
Panjabi	13	11	6	6	0	23	—	—	—
Polish	0	10	0	1	0	9	—	—	—
Serbo-Croat	0	0	1	0	0	1	—	—	—
Spanish	0	0	1	—	—	—	0	0	6
Turkish	—	—	—	—	—	—	0	1	4
Ukrainian	0	2	0	0	0	15	—	—	—
Urdu	6	2	0	13	3	0	—	—	—
Urdu-Arabic	0	0	13	0	0	58	0	2	2
All languages	30	42	34	22	25	136	13	10	120

Key: A Number of classes for which the LEA provides *both* teachers' salaries and accommodation.
B Number of classes for which the LEA provides *either* teachers' salaries *or* accommodation.
C Number of classes for which the LEA provides *neither* teachers' salaries *nor* accommodation.

one started in 1904) the next group is from Eastern Europe, ranging from 1948 to 1955. The Southern European classes begin to appear also in the mid to late 1950s, but most of them date from the 1970s, as do all the Chinese classes. Again, although two of the South Asian groups began in 1957 and one in 1970, all the rest were founded in the last ten years. In Coventry and Bradford it is the South Asian classes which account for more than 80 per cent of the pupils currently attending mother tongue classes, while in Haringey a similar figure applies to the Southern European languages, with Greek alone there representing some 70 per cent of the mother tongue learners located via the MTTD Survey.

One of the main findings of this survey is that the majority of mother tongue classes have no support from the LEA for teacher's salaries or accommodation (see category C in Table 5). Even when those schools or classes receiving some support (usually for the loan of accommodation) are a sizeable number, they are run by, and are the responsibility of, local community organizations or national embassies (category B). And many classes within the curriculum of LEA schools, with teachers paid by the LEA (category A), were set up through the initiative and perseverance of a bilingual teacher in the schools.*

The Mother Tongue Debate

The mother tongue debate, as it is called in England, has focused predominantly on questions of how best to support the existing mother tongue teaching organized by linguistic minorities, and on the most appropriate ways to introduce mother tongue teaching into the state school system. In the early days of the debate these two questions were often presented in discussions as question of 'either/or'. However, subsequent developments in both community-run provision and LEA schooling suggest that both aspects of the question will remain relevant for a long time.

The main questions about provision are perhaps more usefully considered in terms of the long-term objectives on the one hand, and short-term priorities on the other. Even those who see the eventual object to be the incorporation of mother tongue teaching into LEA schools (a view strongly supported by teachers and educationalists actively involved in the debate) are still aware of the present contribution of community-run schools and classes, and they accept the likelihood that in some areas and in the smaller, more geographically scattered linguistic minority populations they will remain the only form of formal teaching. Among the most radical and also the most traditional teachers involved in this debate, there are relatively few who argue for no contact at all with the state system. There are,

---

* Further details of mother tongue teaching provision in Coventry, Bradford and Haringey can be found in Linguistic Minorities Project (1983b); and details of the MTTD Survey Manual for use are available from the National Council for Mother Tongue Teaching, 5 Musgrave Crescent, London SW6.

however, probably sizeable numbers of mother tongue teachers and organizers who would like LEA financial support, but without losing control over the content or organization of their teaching.

These few rather generalized positions represent a much wider range of opinions which are found within a context of restricted options, information and often suspicion or uncertainty. The schemes set up by many LEAs have involved either a relatively small number of pupils, or relatively few hours per week. Tackling just a tiny part of the potential need, as perceived by organizers of community-run provision, these LEA initiatives are rarely seen as a major threat. But often existing tensions between the school authorities and minority organizations are exacerbated by LEA-supported developments which take little account of existing expertise in the local populations, or do not involve the participation of experienced community teachers and others.

There are some other fundamental questions which need to be considered before the very real problems of implementation divert attention away from the wider educational issues involved. What are the educational needs of *monolingual* children growing up in a multilingual neighbourhood, a multilingual society, and an increasingly interdependent world? What is the responsibility of the state *vis-à-vis* the educational rights of *bilingual* children? In the early days of the mother tongue debate in England, the recognition of the educational value of bilingualism for bilinguals focused on suggestions for teaching the languages as examination subjects at secondary school for those pupils who had learned the appropriate language outside school; and for supporting existing community initiatives by, for example, reducing rent for teaching accommodation, or giving small grants for books and materials (but only very rarely were teachers' salaries paid). The justifications for such policies were grounded, first, in principles emerging in multicultural education for recognizing and improving the status of the cultures of ethnic minorities within the school; and, secondly, in discussions about equal opportunity, (a) in education, to develop the pupils' full range of cultural and linguistic resources in the school, and (b) in society, to recognize the right of minorities to develop their own initiatives.

But as the educational proposals were extended to incorporate the treatment of linguistic diversity, language across the curriculum and language awareness for all pupils, the debate also spread to consider the contribution of linguistic and cultural diversity in a range of other subjects, e.g., mathematics, geography. There was a clearer articulation of the role of language in education, and a greater interest in the way the acquisition of more than one language might influence cognitive development and educational achievement as assessed by the official school system. Coupled with the prevailing child-centred pedagogy, it was therefore natural that the mother tongue debate should extend its focus towards appropriate provision for primary school children. This focus was concerned with the socio-psychological and linguistic processes experienced by bilingual children, and it valued the potential resources they brought to a multilingual classroom. But by this time, more participants in the debate argued that the teaching of the languages of minority communities in secondary schools should be a full part of the modern languages curriculum and be open in principle to all pupils — monolingual *or* bilingual.

The latter half of the 1970s and early 1980s was a time of increasing financial cutbacks in education, and of increasingly overt racism in the national and official arenas as well as in local and unofficial situations. Although the strength of educational arguments supporting societal and individual bilingualism was increasingly acknowledged among educationalists and deeply felt by many bilinguals themselves, no substantial effort was initiated to deal with two of the most basic principles underlying a realistic development of mother tongue teaching, whether in LEA or community-run schools, i.e., materials development and teacher training. Despite the setting up of the Schools Council Mother Tongue Materials Project in 1981 and the Royal Society of Arts pilot Certificate in 1983, these questions are still unresolved (Craft and Atkin, 1983), and the very real problems of examinations, deployment of teachers and curriculum development have not been tackled comprehensively. Had this groundwork been developed, the organizational and financial implications might not have proved so inhibiting. Certainly, the non-availability of appropriately trained staff, and the timetabling and financial problems became the main arguments put forward by some administrators and teachers against the introduction of minority languages into LEA schools. Those whose reactions were influenced by assimilationist and, at times, racist views also saw the mother tongue debate as yet another issue concerned with the special 'compensatory' needs of ethnic minority (normally perceived of as black) children. A monolingual perspective reinforced the view that they should assimilate, and that the only practicable way to learn English was to ignore skills in the first language.

There were also other potential conflicts among teachers from both minority and majority backgrounds, who supported the view that questions of minority language teaching should be placed firmly within the framework of education for a multicultural society. Restricted financial resources and lack of political support for education for a multicultural society brought into sharp relief the different priorities of, on the one hand, many ethnic minority and/or mother tongue teachers, impatient with vague commitments and inadequate or no material support for bilingual pupils wishing to retain their first language; and, on the other hand, many other teachers or teacher trainers who were primarily concerned to help monolingual teachers respond to linguistic diversity in the classroom. A more recent tension within the teaching profession is also exacerbated by the economic situation and its undermining of job security. The appointment of mother tongue teachers in LEA schools at a time when there are cutbacks of staff, and in some cases particularly poor results coming from modern language departments, has built up some resentment among some modern language teachers in secondary schools.

For many educationalists actively campaigning in the mother tongue debate, the EEC Directive on the education of migrant worker children was considered marginal if not irrelevant. It was significant in that it showed an official recognition of the importance of mother tongue provision (the actual *right* of an individual child to receive such provision was taken out of the original draft proposal at the insistence of Britain and West Germany). Some educationalists foresaw that such a statement from the European Community would just exacerbate existing governmental hostility to interference in the development of national 'policy', or the functioning of a decentralized system. Other educationalists were suspicious of the economic motives underlying the ideal of a free movement of labour, which is linked in many European countries with migrant labour and insecure citizenship policies for ethnic minorities.

Any assessment of the impact of the Directive needs to consider to whom it was addressed and how it was publicized. Members of the Department of Education and Science often stressed the inappropriateness of the Directive for our decentralized education system, and our settled, no-longer migratory workforce, many of whom are British nationals. However, despite the very real legal and institutional differences, the social and educational experience of the children of migrant and refugee families has some basic similarities. This is an appropriate place to stress that, compared with other European countries, the mother tongue debate in England was increasingly situated within the discussion about education (or more exactly schooling) for all children living in a multicultural society. It is our view, however, that this general area of educational debate and the more specific question of developing the skills of bilingual children should also be firmly grounded in its social context, which involves an analysis of factors beyond the school affecting cultural processes in general and language learning in particular.

The mother tongue debate in England so far has focused on provision of minority language teaching in the later stage of secondary school, or the development of skills in the spoken languages in the early primary school. There has been no serious discussion about the use of two languages as mediums of instruction beyond the very earliest stages of schooling. This, of course, would involve the introduction and development of literacy in both languages throughout the school. It is only recently that the problem of continuity has been discussed linking primary and secondary provision.

Whatever the success of mother tongue provision in teaching the language to younger members of a local linguistic minority, the provision itself is a form of collective activity, often encouraging the continuing use of the 'mother tongue' or 'community language' among the adults involved in organizing it, as well as the pupils themselves. And whatever the objective of the provision, it demonstrates a need that is not being met by the state school system. Even in those LEAs that are appointing bilingual teachers or supporting existing community-run provision, their coverage will in most cases be minimal, supplementing rather than substituting for existing provision. There is no immediate likelihood therefore of state intervention either encouraging or undermining community-run initiatives.[1]

Note

1   This paper has focused on the extent of bilingualism and mother tongue teaching in three cities in England, outlining some of the main features of the mother tongue debate. The summary of our Schools Language Survey findings in five LEAs is now available, and further data will be published as working papers during 1983–85 (obtainable from the Information Office at the London University Institute of Education). The implications of our work for language education policies are discussed in more detail in Linguistic Minorities Project (1983–84). A video for in-service teacher training and teaching materials for primary school children have also been developed by the LINC Project, in collaboration with the ILEA Learning Materials Service and the Schools Council Mother Tongue Project, respectively (LINC, 1983, 1984).

References

AGNIHOTRI, R.K. (1979) *Processes of Assimilation: A Sociolinguistic Study of Sikh Children in Leeds*, DPhil dissertation, University of York.

COMMUNITY LANGUAGES AND EDUCATION PROJECT WORKING PAPERS (1984–85, forthcoming) on the findings of the Adult Language Use Survey.

CRAFT, M. and ATKINS, M. (1983) *Training Teachers of Ethnic Minority Community Languages*, University of Nottingham.

ECONOMIC COMMUNITY'S COUNCIL DIRECTIVE (1977) *On the Education of the Children of Migrant Workers*, Brussels, EEC, 25 July.

HEWITT, R. (1982) 'White adolescent Creole users and the politics of friendship', *Journal of Multilingual and Multicultural Development*.

KHAN, V.S. (1977) *Bilingualism and Linguistic Minorities in Britain: Developments, Perspectives*, London, Runnymede Trust.

KHAN, V.S. (1980) 'The "mother-tongue" of linguistic minorities in multicultural England', *Journal of Multilingual and Multicultural Development*, 1, 1, pp. 71–88.

LINC (Language Information Network Coordination) (1982) *Sharing Languages in the Classroom*, video, available from ILEA Learning Resources Branch, 275 Kennington Lane, London SE11; or from Central Film Library, Bromyard Avenue, London W3. Materials are available from the Children's Language Project, 18 Woburn Square, London WC14 ONS.

LINGUISTIC MINORITIES PROJECT (1983a) *The Schools Language Survey: Summary of Findings from Five LEAs*, LMP/LINC Working Papers Series No. 3, available from Information Office, University of London, Institute of Education, 20 Bedford Way, London.

LINGUISTIC MINORITIES PROJECT (1983b, forthcoming) *Summary of the Mother-Tongue Teaching Directory Survey Findings* in LMP/LINC Working Paper Series, Information Office, Institute of Education, 20 Bedford Way, London.

LINGUISTIC MINORITIES PROJECT (1983c, forthcoming) *Summary of Full Report to the Department of Education and Science*, Autumn, enquiries to LINC 18 Woburn Square, London.

LINGUISTIC MINORITIES PROJECT (1984, forthcoming) *The Other Languages of England*, London, Routledge and Kegan Paul.

NATIONAL CONGRESS ON LANGUAGES IN EDUCATION (1983) *Minority Community Languages in School*, NCLE Papers and Reports 4, CILT.

TOSI, A. (1979) 'Mother tongue teaching for the children of migrants', *Language Teaching and Linguistics Abstracts*, 12, 4, pp. 213–31.

WILDING J. (1981) *Ethnic Minority Languages in the Classroom?* Leicester, Leicester Council for Community Relations and Leicester City Council.

WILLEY R. and HOULTON, D. (1982) *Supporting Children's Bilingualism*, London, Schools Council.

Minority Pupil Progress

Peter Figueroa

The 'underachievement' of minority pupils has been regularly re-ported for some years, but in this analysis Dr Figueroa critically reviews the methodology, findings and policy implications of these studies.

Over the past two decades, there have been persistent reports of educational 'underachievement' among ethnic minority children of Caribbean and Asian origin, and particularly among the former. But such research as has been undertaken leaves many questions un-answered, and this paper seeks to review the situation with particular reference to pupils of Caribbean background. What are the research findings? How are they to be interpreted? How is the existing situation to be accounted for, and what action seems necessary?

There will be no attempt here to give a comprehensive review of the literature, as such reviews are already to be found elsewhere, for instance, F. Taylor (1974), Tomlinson (1980) and M. Taylor (1981). However, some of the main findings and some recent and less well-known studies will be briefly reviewed. It is hoped that this will provide a picture of what seems to be the situation. But beyond that, the intention is to highlight some of the important issues which require attention. The aim is to offer a critical appraisal, and, in particular, to stress the need for a closer scrutiny of research methodologies and findings in this vital area of educational policy.

Three Literature Reviews

F. Taylor (1974) reviewed the literature up to the early 1970s. Among other things she considered English language education, cultural factors and 'problems' in determining the ability and academic potential of 'immigrant' children. The perspectives of disadvantage, deprivation, culture clash, home background and compensatory education seem predominant.

Tomlinson (1980) summarized, with minimal comment, a series of studies ranging from about 1966 to 1980. Of these, thirty-three dealt with West Indian, and nineteen with Asian, 'educational performance'. She concludes that twenty-six of the thirty-three studies concerning West Indians (that is, 79 per cent) show West Indian children 'to score lower than white children on individual or group tests or to be over-represented in ESN schools and under-represented in higher school streams.' The other seven studies (21 per cent) show West Indians doing as well as or better than whites. Of the nineteen studies concerned with Asians, twelve (63 per cent) indicated 'a lower score than whites on individual or group tests, or slightly fewer O/CSE passes than whites'. The other seven studies (37 per cent) have Asians doing at least as well as whites. Her conclusions suggest that both Asian and West Indian children, but particularly the latter, are 'performing' less well than whites.

Tomlinson tends to report the studies she summarized at face value, declining to enter into the debate over 'culture-fair' assessment, or to highlight the serious problems with teacher assessment, which was used in many of the studies. Thus her 'neutral' and 'factual' review of the literature could actually be misleading.

M. Taylor (1981) reviews a wide range of research studies from about 1965 to about 1980 on the 'attainment and performance' of pupils of West Indian origin in the areas of language (Standard British English) and reading; mathematics; and other curricular activities, such as sport, music, dance and drama. She also considers studies concerned with Creole, school placement, examinations, overrepresentation in ESN schools, ability, and 'behavioural deviance' and psychiatric disorders (highlighting the pathological model at the basis of her approach).

She also reviews studies on home and school factors which might help account for the 'attainment and performance' of the pupils of West Indian origin. In particular, she considers the attitudes, perceptions, aspirations and expectations of parents, pupils (both West Indians and their peers) and teachers. She gives a good deal of importance to alleged problems of self-identity and self-esteem among West Indians, asserting that 'self-esteem' (in this context, problems with self-esteem' 'is obviously [sic] a crucial and pivotal concept in understanding the position of pupils of West Indian origin in schools' (p. 207). Although she lists Stone (1981) in her bibliography, she does not consider Stone's arguments against this view. Similarly, although she summarizes (pp. 181–2) some aspects of Figueroa (1974, 1976), she does not mention that he found evidence (pp. 386–92) of positive self-image among the West Indians of school-leaving age he studied. Nor does she seem aware of the reservations that can be made about the mechanistic way in which the development of self-concept and its relation to achievement have often been understood. For instance, Figueroa (1974, pp. 387–8) observes:

'it would . . . be unwarranted to assume that a subordinated group would necessarily have a thoroughly negative group-self-image . . . the subordinate group's image of itself . . . will also depend on the dynamics within the group. . . . Of course, the inter- and the intra-group dynamics which influence [note: not "determine"] the self-image and the image of the other are themselves closely interrelated.'

Taylor does consider the issue of institutionalized racism — but this is the only factor she presents with a query point. Furthermore, she discusses in some detail the problematic nature of the concepts and measures of ability and achievement; yet she proceeds to treat at face value many of the studies which are conceptually and methodologically problematical in precisely such terms — except, in particular, when discussing evidence of teacher racism. Thus, after reviewing evidence of teachers' negative stereotypes and attitudes regarding West Indians, she grants that 'it appears from research evidence that the attitudes of teachers, and hence probably their expectations, are likely to be of considerable influence on the performance of children of West Indian origin' (p. 206). But she hastens to stress 'that many of the research studies reviewed here tap only crude measures of teachers' attitudes' (*ibid.*). She thus proffers, instead, the unsubstantiated *opinions* that the reservations of many of the teachers about 'a multicultural curriculum *may well* be for professional . . . reasons' (*ibid.*, my emphasis); and, 'it is by no means to be assumed that they are racialist. . . .' Yet, no reservations are expressed when she claims, on very slim evidence, that ' . . . the general trend of this review would suggest that . . . the attitudes of white children to their black peers . . . and their behaviour especially towards West Indians . . . seem generally to be favourable' (*op. cit.*, p. 193).

Peter Figueroa

Ethnic Minority Pupil Placement

Let us consider the evidence on the location of ethnic minority pupils (especially those of Caribbean background) within the educational system, first, by type of school, and then within schools.

National data are sparse and often tend to provide limited, survey-type information. Other studies have been local, small-scale investigations. Both national and local studies have often employed problematical methodologies and instruments.

One of the earliest national studies is reported by Townsend (1971). He found (pp. 56ff), on the basis of DES figures for 1970, that Asians and especially Caribbeans were grossly underrepresented among pupils in selective, academic oriented secondary education (see Table 1).

Table 1. Black and White Pupils in Maintained Grammar and ESN Schools in England, January 1970

		Grammar		ESN	
		Percentage	Total	Percentage	Total
1	Blacks (3–5 below)	2.6	60,959	1.5	185,812
2	White British	20.3	2,957,167	0.7	7,214,968
3	Caribbean	1.6	31,320	2.3	109,580
4	Pakistani	2.5	10,202	0.4	23,995
5	Indian	3.9	19,437	0.3	52,237

Source: Townsend (1971), Tables 5.2 and 5.1.

One of the first studies of West Indian school-leavers in Britain was carried out by Figueroa (1974). He collected information in 1966–67 from 261 white British, 88 West Indian, 48 Cypriot and 33 'other' fourth, fifth, and (a few) sixth formers in ten secondary modern schools in Haringey, north London. He discovered that the ethnic minority pupils in that borough were greatly underrepresented in selective secondary education (see Table 2).

At the other extreme, Townsend (1971) also found that pupils of Caribbean origin were substantially overrepresented nationally in schools for the educationally subnormal (ESN schools), while Asians were underrepresented there (Table 1). In 1966 in the Inner London Education Authority (ILEA) 'immigrants' comprised 23.3 per cent of pupils in ESN schools, but only 13.2 per cent of the school population as a whole (ILEA, 1967). In 1967 the figures were 28 per

Table 2. Black and White Pupils in Maintained Grammar Schools in
Haringey, January 1967

		Percentage	Total
1	White British	41.1	11,782
2	Caribbean	2.9	941
3	Cypriots	5.6	815
4	Indian and Pakistani	16.8	173

Source: Figueroa (1974), Table 2.7–9

cent (of which 75 per cent were West Indian) and 15 per cent
respectively, (ILEA, 1968b; Omar, 1971). Fethney (1973) reported
that by 1972 'immigrants' in Inner London represented 31 per cent of
the ESN school rolls even though they accounted for only 17 per cent
of the total school population.

Tomlinson (1982) found that by 1972 the national figure for
Caribbeans in ESN(M) schools and classes was 2.9 per cent of all
relevant Caribbean pupils, a substantial increase on the 1970 figure
given by Townsend. By contrast, the percentage of pupils as a whole
in ESN(M) schools and classes in 1972 seemed about the same as, or
just a little down on, 1970. Besides the ESN question, another
disturbing issue has also recently gained attention: that of the
overrepresentation of Caribbean children in the popularly termed 'sin
bins', ('disruptive units' and the like) although few relevant data are
available. (See, for instance, Tomlinson, 1980.)

As regards the location of ethnic minority pupils *within* schools,
Townsend and Brittan (1972) found in 1971 in a study of 230 schools
as part of the national project mentioned above, that both in primary
and secondary schools where there was streaming the Asian and
Caribbean children (but particularly the latter) tended to be clustered
in the lower streams (see Figueroa, 1974, Table 2.7–14). It is hardly
surprising, therefore, that their figures for 1970 show that in the fifth
forms studied as many as 23 per cent of Caribbeans, 26 per cent of
Indians and 32 per cent of Pakistanis were taking *non-examination*
courses, compared with only 3 per cent of the white British pupils,
while only 6 per cent of Asians and Caribbeans, compared with 42
per cent of white British, were taking GCE O-level courses (Townsend and Brittan, 1972).

Figueroa (1974, Table 7.8) in the study referred to above had
found evidence of Caribbean and especially Cypriot pupils not only

being concentrated in secondary modern schools, but also clustering in the lower streams in those non-selective schools. He also found in 1967 in his matched follow-up subsample (twenty-one white British boys, twenty-one Caribbean boys, twenty-two white British girls, twenty-two Caribbean girls — matched for school class and sex) that 86 per cent of both the white and the Caribbean boys, 41 per cent of the white girls and 50 per cent of the Caribbean girls had obtained no school-leaving qualifications whatsoever. (Girls often did Pitmans or RSA examinations.) It should, of course, be borne in mind here that the majority of Caribbean pupils in Haringey at this time were in the schools studied, whereas over 40 per cent of white British pupils were in selective schools.

Pupil 'Achievement': Earlier Studies

Another source of national data on the situation of ethnic minority pupils is the National Child Development Study (Davie *et al.*, 1972), although the numbers of such children in this study were relatively small (77 West Indian, at age 7; and 121 West Indian and 72 Asian at age 11, compared with over 10,000 white British in both age groups). This was a longitudinal study of all children in England, Scotland and Wales born 3–9 March 1958. Information was collected at birth and when the children were aged 7, 11 and 16, and was based on teachers' reports and assessment, on educational test data and tests of achievement, and on responses by parents, the children themselves, doctors and health visitors. Bagley (1982), who has analyzed in detail the data on children of immigrant parents (black and white) at ages 7 and 11 concluded (p. 115) that 'the educational data at age 7 show under-achievement by all of the children of immigrant parents; but the West Indian children in particular seem to show massive underachievement.' At age 11 (when more children born abroad were included), the Caribbean and Asian children compared badly with the white British children.

The Educational Priority Areas action research of the 1960s is another large-scale project which provides some information about Caribbean and Asian pupils (Halsey, 1972; Barnes, 1975; and especially Payne, 1974). The relevant data concern primary school children in London (Deptford) and Birmingham, both areas of 'high concentration of immigrants' — which was, interestingly, one of the official criteria of disadvantage of British-born children. Tests administered included the English Picture Vocabulary Tests (EPVT, levels I and II), which are tests of listening vocabulary, and the SRA reading abilities test. The mean EPVT (level I and II) scores of 5–6 and 7–10-year olds, and the mean SRA scores of 8–10-year-olds were as shown in Table 3. These scores are all below the national norms, which is hardly surprising since the tests were carried out in EPA schools, that is, in disadvantaged areas. Furthermore, the mean scores of the Caribbean pupils were consistently lower than those of the white British pupils, and those of the Asians were the lowest of all.

Table 3. EPA Mean EPVT and SRA Scores

	White British		Caribbeans		Asians	
		(n)		(n)		(n)
1 *EPVT level I:*						
Ages 5–6						
London	97.9	(957)	86.9	(298)	—	—
Birmingham	89.5	(342)	81.6	(96)	69.6	(121)
2 *EPVT level II:*						
Ages 7–10						
London	92.9	(1162)	84.5	(250)	—	—
Birmingham	86.4	(785)	80.1	(209)	72.7	(373)
3 *SRA: Ages 8–10*						
London	93.0	(878)	88.1	(161)	—	—
Birmingham	86.4	(360)	83.5	(107)	78.4	(173)

Source: Payne (1974), Figure A(1–6).

Another relatively large-scale study was undertaken in 1966 by the Inner London Education Authority (ILEA, 1968a). This was concerned with 11+ transfer in fifty-two ILEA primary schools with a high proportion of 'immigrants'. The 'immigrant' pupils transferring from these schools numbered 1068, over half of whom were West Indian. The data were obtained from a verbal reasoning test, teachers' assessment of English and mathematics, and heads' responses (all of which are problematical measures). Whereas half of the white British pupils were rated as below average, as one would expect on a normal distribution, four-fifths of the 'immigrant' children were so rated — and the West Indian children specifically were rated somewhat worse.

Two other ILEA studies were carried out in 1968 (Little, 1975). The first of these used a sentence completion test of reading ability with 32,000 8-year-olds. This cohort was tested again for literacy at ages 10 and 15. But by the last testing there had been substantial wasting of the cohort. The average score for respondents as a whole was below the national norm (100) — which might indicate something about the schools concerned — but the 'immigrants' scored worse than the white British, and the West Indians scored on average worst of all. The scores in the three years for the white British and the West Indians were as shown in Table 4.

Table 4. *Mean Reading Scores at 8, 10 and 15 years (ILEA Literacy Survey)*

Age	White British	West Indian
8	98.1	88.1
10	98.3	87.4
15	97.8	85.9
Numbers	12,530	1,465

Source: Rampton Report (1981), p. 20.

The other ILEA study in 1968 investigated the 'performance' of 4269 'immigrant' and 22,023 white British pupils aged 11. Again the 'immigrants' did worse than the white British, and the West Indians worst of all.

Another fairly large-scale study (Yule *et al.*, 1975) carried out in 1970, again in London, tested the total 10-year-old maintained school population in one borough: 2281 pupils, including 354 Caribbeans. The NFER non-verbal IQ test, NV5, and the SRA reading abilities test were used. Teachers also rated the children's behaviour. Mean scores were generally below the national norms, which might again be a reflection of the characteristics of the schools concerned. The white British scored consistently better than the minority children (who included Cypriots), and the Caribbean pupils tended on average to score the lowest, with those born in the West Indies doing the worst on the test of non-verbal reasoning. A subsample of fifty-one UK-born Caribbean children and forty-nine born in the West Indies and 105 white British children was also given individual tests. The white British tended to score significantly better, with the West Indian-born children coming out the worst on reading ability.

More Recent Studies

The most recent fairly extensive information available is based on the DES 1978/79 school-leavers survey for six selected local education authorities, covering about half of the 'ethnic minority' school-leavers in England (DES, 1981). These are, therefore, boroughs with high concentrations of Asian and Caribbean pupils. Similar DES statistics for 1981/82 have also been provided for the Swann Commit-tee, but at the time of writing they had not been published. However, they seem largely to confirm those for 1978/79, which showed the Caribbean leavers to be poorly placed educationally at the higher levels (see Table 5). It should be noted, however, that as a group the Caribbean leavers are actually doing well at the lower levels (Table 5.1). Overall, for all examinations, a larger proportion of the West Indians than of either the Asians or other leavers in the six LEAs was successful in obtaining *some* graded results at CSE and O-level. It may be the case, not that the failure rate among the Caribbean candidates is particularly high, but that Caribbean pupils are often not channelled towards the more academic, higher status GCE examinations. Specific large-scale data on this question, including pass rates for GCE, should be enlightening.

As only a small proportion of West Indians are being funnelled through to success at A-level, it is not surprising that such a small proportion of them seems to be going on to university. However, to judge from Tables 5.2 and 5.3 it would seem that compared with all other leavers, a much larger proportion of the Caribbean leavers who do obtain A-levels are going on to university.

On the whole, the available data (Table 5) do indicate that the Asians are quite well placed — though still not generally as well as the white British nationally, except for overall A-level results. Yet, of those leavers who obtained A-levels, a smaller proportion of Asians than of white British nationality seem to get into university (Tables 5.2 and 5.3).

Craft and Craft (1983) carried out a study in 1979 of all fifth year and second year sixth formers in an Outer London borough with a high concentration of ethnic minority pupils. Of a total of almost 3000 children, the sample included 248 West Indian and 568 Asian fifth formers, but only 9 West Indian and 135 Asian second year sixth formers. The researchers found (Table 6) that the Asians did less well than the white British at A-level, even when controlled for social class, but better than the West Indians (although *their* sixth form numbers were very small and this finding is therefore inconclusive). It

Table 5.   Leavers in Six LEAs, 1978/79

		Asians[1]	WI[1]	Others	Totals[2] for England
				(percentages)	
1	*CSE and O-Level Results*				
	English:				
	Ungraded/Not taken[3]	32	30	30	21
	All graded results	69	70	70	79
	Higher grades[4]	21	9	29	34
	Mathematics:				
	Ungraded/Not taken[3]	39	48	40	32
	All graded results	62	52	61	68
	Higher grades[4]	20	5	19	23
	All Examinations:				
	Ungraded/Not taken[3]	19	17	22	14
	All graded results	81	84	78	87
	Higher grades[4]	18	3	16	21
2	*A-Level Results*				
	No pass/Not taken[3]	87	98	88	87
	One or more passes	13	2	12	13
3	*Destination*				
	University	3	1	3	5
	Other HE/FE[5]	18	16	9	14
	Employment	54	65	77	74
	Unknown[6]	25	18	11	8
	Numbers	527	799	4852	693,840

Source: DES (1981), Tables A–E (adapted).
Notes: 1 No details are given in the Rampton Report of how the Asians and West Indians were identified as such.
   2 That is, school leavers from all maintained schools in England based on a 10 per cent sample survey.
   3 Although this has not been made clear throughout, these figures appear, from Table C, to include not only candidates who obtained no graded results (or in the case of A-levels, 'passes') in the examinations, but also those leavers who were not entered for the examinations concerned.
   4 'Higher grades' are defined as grades A–C at O-level and grade 1 CSE.
   5 Table E in the Rampton Report simply distinguishes between 'University' and 'Other further education'. From the context it would appear that the latter includes all non-university higher education — as well as further education.
   6 Presumably 'Unknown' includes the unemployed, though this is not mentioned in the Rampton Report.

would seem (*ibid.*, Table 5) that a much larger proportion of the West Indians than of the white British or Asian fifth formers went on to further education, rather than into the sixth form, even when controlled for social class and level of GCE O-level performance. Unfortunately, no information is available about their performance there, for further education certainly acts as an alternative route to university for some West Indians, and most of these pupils had achieved good levels in GCE/CSE. The GCE/CSE O-level results of the Asian fifth formers, controlled for social class, were very similar to those of the white British, while those of the West Indians were poorer (*ibid.*, Table 2). None of the nine West Indian second year sixth formers went on to a university or a polytechnic, and Asians were rather less likely than white British to go into higher education, and in particular to a university (*ibid.*, Table 9).

In a case study of one small comprehensive school with about 50 per cent Asian and 10 per cent Caribbean pupils, funded by the Commission for Racial Equality (see Figueroa and Swart, 1982), the researchers found that ethnic minority candidates generally tend to take more examination papers than the white British. Also, in both the GCE O-level and the CSE examinations, the results of the Asian pupils, the only large group of ethnic minority pupils, are comparable to those of their white British school peers. There are, however, variations between the different Asian groups. The school is situated in the inner city of a provincial town, and the pupils are, by and large, of a working-class background. Only preliminary results are available so far, and it is not yet possible to say how these results compare with those for the city as a whole. In 1980 there were only six West Indian pupils in the fifth year, and, in contrast with their Asian and white British peers, none of them was entered for O-levels. However, five of them took between them thirty CSE papers — an average of six per candidate compared with the overall average in the school of just under four papers per candidate. They obtained between them twenty-six results graded 2–4, but, unlike the Asians and the white British, no grade 1 passes.

In the 1982 O-level examinations, eleven out of the fifteen Asian candidates, and ten out of the thirteen white British, obtained at least one grade A-C, but with both the Asians and white British obtaining on average about two passes per candidate. There were only seven West Indian pupils in the fifth year. Only two were entered for O-levels and they received one grade A-C between them. Six of the West Indians were entered for CSE, taking twenty-nine papers between them (an average of 4.8 each, the overall average in the school being

4.7). They obtained a mean of 4.0 graded results each, compared with 3.9 for the white British and 4.3 for the Asians. However, none of these Caribbean pupils obtained any grade 1 results, as against 22 per cent of the white British and 28 per cent of the Asian candidates.

Some Counter Evidence

The majority of the studies reviewed above suggest that ethnic minority pupils, especially those of Caribbean background, are not very well placed within the British educational system. However, some studies indicate a favourable situation, both on tests of 'ability' and on various measures of attainment.

Bagley (1982) in his re-analysis of the National Child Development Study already referred to, found that some Caribbean pupils came out very well on the Draw-a-Man test used to identify gifted children. In 1965, when the children were 7 years old, a higher proportion (4 per cent) of the Caribbean pupils than of pupils in *any* of the other ethnic groups, including the white British, fell in the highly gifted group.

Houghton (1966) administered a Stanford-Binet intelligence test to seventy-one matched pairs of Caribbean and white British infant school children. There was no significant difference between the mean scores of the Caribbean children (90.09) and those of the white British (92.00) — although these scores were below the national norm, the research having been carried out in the deprived inner city areas of Nottingham. In a partial replication of Houghton (1966), Bagley (1971) gave a Stanford-Binet intelligence test to fifty matched pairs of Caribbean and white British primary school children of stable working-class or lower middle-class homes in London. Both sets of children had scores above the national norm, the Caribbean children having a mean of 105.7 and the white British 103.2. This difference was not statistically significant.

Wiles (1968) found in one ILEA comprehensive school that 'immigrant' children who had had all of their schooling in the UK performed as well as the white British. 'Immigrants' were, besides, somewhat more likely to be in the top streams. In another study of fifty-nine black London primary school children mainly of middle-class background, Bagley (1975) again found that children (judged to be) of pure African or mixed African and European descent scored above the national norm on a Stanford-Binet test. Stones (1979), in a study of thirty Caribbean and thirty white British junior children in a

Midlands inner city school, found that there was little difference in the performance of the two groups on the Raven's Progressive Matrices Test, as long as the children had been taught with materials based on the same principles contained in the test.

Craft and Craft (1983), in the 1979 study reported above, found that white British fifth formers were well behind all other ethnic groups in continuing in full-time education, at each level of performance in CSE/GCE O-level; and that Asians were well ahead at all levels except the highest, where West Indians marginally had the lead (Table 3). Furthermore, while middle-class fifth formers were less likely to leave full-time education in all ethnic groups, among pupils from working-class families Asians were well ahead of their peers with almost 80 per cent deciding to stay on in full-time education (Table 4).

Rutter (1982) reported CSE and GCE results for examinations taken in the fifth and up to the end of the sixth form between 1976 and 1978 by pupils in twelve non-selective Inner London schools, a subset of a cohort of pupils who were originally studied at age 10 (Yule, 1975 — see above). He found that, altogether, the Caribbeans did slightly better than whites:

> 26 per cent had 1 to 4 'O' levels compared with 24 per cent of whites, and a further 19 per cent had 5 or more 'O' levels compared with 11 per cent of whites ... only 18 per cent of blacks left school without any graded passes in CSE or 'O' levels, compared with 34 per cent of whites.

He accounted for this above all in terms of 'the greater commitment to education shown by the black pupils'. Their attendance in the fifth year was better, they were less likely to leave school at Easter and more likely to stay into the sixth form.

Driver (1980) carried out a study of the combined GCE O-level and CSE examination results in 1975–77 of 2310 16-year-old school-leavers from five inner city schools. Of these school-leavers 590 were Caribbean. Driver found that on the whole these, especially the girls, did somewhat better than their white British school peers. It must be noted, however, not only that Driver's sample cannot be taken to be representative (as is the case in a number of studies claiming Caribbean 'underachievement'); but also that the unit system he used to score various levels of passes probably tended to inflate the value of lower level results and to deflate that of the higher level passes. In any case, even though these Caribbean leavers as a whole may be doing somewhat better than their white British school peers, their performance was still not as good as their peers nationally (Taylor, 1981, p. 121).

Nevertheless, Driver's study does remind us that even if *generally* and *on average* the situation of Caribbean pupils in Britain is not very good, the matter is complex and it is difficult to discuss it without oversimplifying and falling into stereotypes. Some Caribbeans certainly do very well within the British educational system. Moreover, the various studies finding that Caribbean pupils are poorly placed themselves suffer from certain shortcomings and limitations, some of which will now be briefly considered.

Limitations in Methodology

As should be apparent from the research literature reviewed in this chapter so far, many of the studies are local, small-scale enquiries, carried out in urban areas — indeed in inner cities — with high proportions of ethnic minorities. The majority have been carried out in London. Many (although not all) seem to rely on 'opportunity samples', and to be rather basic in design and methodology, often failing, for instance, to control adequately or at all for social class (see M. Taylor, 1981, pp. 210ff). It cannot on the whole therefore be assumed that the findings of these studies are representative. At best they probably provide a picture only of the most disadvantaged pupils. Even the larger-scale projects tend to refer to London (e.g., the ILEA studies and part of the EPA projects) or at least to urban boroughs with high proportions of ethnic minorities (e.g., the DES six LEAs project). Yet almost half of the West Indian population lives outside Greater London (CRE, 1978), and probably a significant minority outside the conurbations.

There are also many problems with the measures and instruments used in the various studies. The difficulties and issues cannot be fully discussed here, but a number are considered below and others are reviewed by M. Taylor (1981). First of all there is the odd definition of 'immigrant' pupils which the DES previously used. 'Immigrant' pupils included children born in the UK (!) to parents who had come to Britain not more than ten years previously (!!) — thus excluding increasingly more and more black English children as the years passed. Moreover, in practice this definition may well have resulted in a good deal of unreliability in the returns made by heads: did they always have or seek reliable information on the date of parents' arrival in the UK? The net effect may well have been to exclude from the statistics a good many children who were quite well-placed educationally. Perhaps this affected Caribbean pupils in particular, since the Caribbean migration predated that from the Indian subcontinent and especially the more middle-class migration of East African Indians.

Another point is that some studies have relied on teachers to categorize pupils, sometimes retrospectively, into different ethnic groups. This could lead to the omission of Caribbean pupils who did not correspond to the general stereotypes.

Perhaps more serious is that many measures, for instance measures of attainment or linguistic competence, rely on teacher assessment (see below). This could lead to unreliability and bias, especially in view of findings such as those by Brittan (1976) and Tomlinson (1982) that teachers and heads tend to have academically and behaviourally unfavourable stereotypes of Caribbean pupils. There is also the problem of 'intelligence tests', the very notion of 'general intelligence' being a cultural construct, and problematical (see below).

Some of the research studies of 'underachievement' are undoubtedly of limited or uncertain validity and generalizability. Nevertheless, it seems clear that in terms of the criteria relied on within the British school system — for example, mainstream schools versus ESN schools, GCE versus CSE — a relatively large proportion of Caribbean pupils is not very well placed.

However, the question which arises here is how this is to be understood. Is it most appropriate, as is commonly the case, to conceptualize the matter in terms of 'underachievement'? Or would it be more accurate to speak of the educational inequality of ethnic minorities — in particular, of Caribbean pupils — and of the British educational system's failure in this respect?

Underachievement or Inequality?

To speak of the 'underachievement' of Caribbean pupils is to make several questionable assumptions, and inclines one to account for the situation in terms of individual and pathological pupil characteristics such as supposedly low ability, low motivation, self-concept problems, linguistic deprivation, and deprived or problematical home and cultural backgrounds. Assumptions about at least the following seem to be built into a conceptualization in terms of 'underachievement':

1 ability, and, more precisely, 'general intelligence';
2 the existence of valid, reliable and culture-fair measures of such ability or 'general intelligence';
3 the existence of valid, reliable and culture-fair measures of attainment;
4 the opportunity to learn and to perform (including being taught appropriately with appropriate materials and through appropriate curricula).

The very notion of fixed and determinable levels of ability and, in particular, of 'general intelligence' is problematic. Intelligence is not a talent buried in the ground, but a living relationship that alters and develops (see Vernon, 1969).

But even if one accepted the trivial definition that intelligence is what intelligence tests measure, there would still be questions about whether the same intelligence test measures the same characteristic in different individuals, especially individuals from different cultures and linguistic groups, and also whether it measures it with the same efficiency. More technically, tests like the modified Stanford-Binet test have not been standardized on Caribbean and Asian populations in the UK (Verma and Mallick, 1982), and tend to be culturally and linguistically biased to the detriment of such pupils. (On the cultural and ideological bias built into such tests see, for instance, Karier, 1976; Kamin, 1977.) For example, the EPA project in London included the Illinois Test of Psycholinguistic Abilities, which used American norms. Also, this and other tests depend largely on skills of listening, yet those administering the test are no doubt usually Standard British English speakers, and not Caribbean or Asian.

Measures of attainment suffer no less from lack of appropriate standardization and from cultural and linguistic bias. Indeed, in several of the studies reviewed above, teacher assessment was relied on. For instance, in the ILEA transfer study (Little *et al.*, 1968), teachers' assessments were used for attainment in mathematics. Teacher assessment and teacher opinion also represented a substantial part of the data collected in the National Child Development Study. For their part, CSE and GCE examination boards seem so far to have paid scant attention to the problem of cultural bias, whether in the content or in the form and context of the questions. But recently there seem to be some hopeful developments. (See, for instance, Lashley, 1979; Schools Council, 1981; and Vida and Figueroa, 1983.)

The final assumption is perhaps not one that is often recognized. The question which needs, above all, to be asked is to do with whether ethnic minority children, and especially those of Caribbean background, have really had fair educational opportunities and rigorous teaching (see Stone, 1981). As we have seen, many children certainly seem to be in an unequal position within the educational system, overrepresented at its bottom end, and underrepresented among those receiving high level school-leaving qualifications — and hence also underrepresented among those going on into higher education.

To conceptualize the available information in terms of educational inequality rather than simply of individual underachievement directs one's attention to the structural and institutional realities within which the situation of these ethnic minority pupils, and especially the Caribbeans, needs to be understood. The way in which the educational system is structured and operates with respect to these pupils' needs to be seen within — but not as simply determined by — the structure and dynamics of the wider society. However, my concern here is more restricted, and the specific question which arises is how, and to what extent, one may account for the educational inequality of Caribbean pupils, in particular in terms of the structure and workings of the educational system itself.

Accounting for the Situation

In the literature a range of factors has been considered in trying to account for the situation of ethnic minority children, especially the Caribbeans, within the British educational system and these have been reviewed in particular by M. Taylor (1981). The approach in these accounts has mostly tended to be atomistic in at least two senses. First, the factors have often been treated as isolable and as functioning independently, rather than in an interactive way. Secondly, there has been a stress on supposed individual characteristics. Moreover, research accounts have often been set within a pathological perspective; that is, there has tended to be a search for what might be 'wrong' with, or 'problematical', 'deficient' or 'deviant' about ethnic minority children, in particular the Caribbeans, and about their backgrounds.

Thus Caribbean pupils' supposed identity, self-concept and self-esteem problems have been much emphasized, and related to supposed problems in motivation. Cultural factors have also been highlighted. Attention has been focused on 'migration shock', 'culture shock', degree of identification with the 'host' community, child-minding patterns, 'female dominance', and other aspects of family life and family organization. Parents' and pupils' attitudes towards education have sometimes been thought to be negative or inadequate, although evidence to the contrary has been provided by Figueroa (1974), Rex and Tomlinson (1979), Stone (1981), Rutter (1982) and others. Sometimes the focus has been on adjustment to British educational practices, differences between home and school (especially with respect to discipline), parents' educational background, pupils' early education, length of education in Britain, and length of stay in Britain. Supposed 'language problems' and 'linguistic deprivation' have also received attention. Socio-economic background has been considered too, but mainly within the context of social disadvantage and along with related factors such as quality of accommodation.

Factors that relate more to the educational system and which have received some attention include inappropriate tests, context of testing (such as colour of tester), and teachers' attitudes, stereotypes and expectations. The notion of institutional racism has been put forward more recently.

However, there is still a dearth of substantial and sophisticated research into how the structures and processes of the educational system and of individual schools might be failing to facilitate the full academic development of Caribbean pupils. It could be argued that it is up to the school, and the educational system as a whole, to adapt to the pupils. The school can hardly hope effectively to fulfil its task of enabling pupils to acquire the necessary skills, knowledge, attitudes and ways of behaving unless it is able to make contact with the pupils on their wave-length, and to start from where they are. Important as the classroom teacher is in the school process, the issue here is not just to do with the individual teacher. How do the policies — or lack of coherent, stated policies — of (among others) the DES, the LEAs, the professional associations, and the examination boards, fundamentally influence the opportunities of ethnic minority children, especially the Caribbeans? What of the practices of such bodies? What strategies — if any — do they have for implementing and evaluating the working of their policies? What of the staffing, organizaion and ethos of the schools? What of the typical curriculum and its ethnocentrism? What of the teaching materials? What of the assessment and placement procedures? What educational opportunities, experiences and teaching do Caribbean pupils typically receive? What, also, of the attitudes, stereotypes, expectations and ignorance of many of the teachers and white British pupils? And what of the lack of training of the teachers — which has recently been a focus of discussion and documentation (Craft, 1981; DES, 1981; Eggleston, *et al.*, 1981; and House of Commons, 1981)?

Although adequate research evidence is not available on most such questions, there are nevertheless some pointers. For instance, Craft and Craft (1983), discussed above, have found that although a large proportion of Caribbean pupils stay on in full-time education beyond the fifth form, more of these than among their peers transfer to further education rather than remaining in school. Could this reflect on the treatment or situation of Caribbeans in mainstream schools?

Again, in both the EPA and one of the ILEA projects mentioned above, there is some evidence that, compared with white British pupils, the reading scores of Caribbean pupils in British schools are more likely to become worse over the years of schooling (Payne, 1974; Little, 1975; Mabey, 1981). Clearly, at best, this does not signal a success for that schooling; and it may be directly related to various school processes.

First of all, the issues of culture and language bias, and in general of the validity and reliability of measures touched on earlier, apply not only to research. More crucially, they also apply to the tests and assessment procedures and throughout a child's school career. The overrepresentation of Caribbean children in ESN schools referred to above seems to illustrate this. Coard, a West Indian, was the first to discuss the ILEA (1967) figures which provide some evidence to suggest that this overrepresentation could be the result of school processes, and in particular of the assessment procedures (Coard, 1971). These ILEA statistics in fact indicate a significant incidence of misplacement of Caribbean pupils into ESN schools. Coard also shows from the same report that only a very small proportion of such children ever return to normal schools; once misplaced, their chances of a (relatively) high status education are, in practice, for the most part, irrevocably — and unjustly — denied. It may not be insignificant that some white British researchers have apparently found it necessary to minimize Coard's work by labelling it 'emotive', 'polemical', 'anecdotal', 'not research', and a 'short book' (see, for instance, Tomlinson, 1980; Taylor, 1981).

One could reasonably hypothesize, too, that less dramatic misplacement, misplacement into lower and non-academic streams for instance, also occurs to a disproportionate extent among Caribbean pupils, and — especially when it occurs at a relatively early age — likewise tends to have a long-term and academically damaging outcome. Related to this is what has been referred to as 'channelling'. For instance, Carrington (1983, p. 61) concludes on the basis of a case study of an 11–16 inner city comprehensive school in Yorkshire, 'that the overrepresentation of West Indian pupils in school sports teams is, in part, the outcome of channelling by teachers' of such pupils out of the academic mainstream and into sport.

Furthermore, the stereotyping of Caribbean pupils would seem to play an important part in such misassessment, misplacement and channelling, as well as in other aspects of schooling. Thus, Tomlinson (1982), in a study concerning forty children passing into special education (only eighteen of whom were of 'immigrant parentage'), and including interviews with thirty heads and with various other professionals, found evidence which suggests that the ESN misplacement of Caribbean pupils is at least partly the outcome of stereotyping. Heads had stereotypes of Caribbean pupils which correspond to the criteria they use for ESN placement. Heads also tended to stereotype Asians, but in ways which did not have similar negative educational implications. For instance, heads considered that West Indian children were 'bound to be slower — it's their personalities' (p. 164); whereas, 'the functional problems' of Asian children 'were considered to be related to language' (p. 168). Tomlinson concludes (p. 167) that 'the actual referral and assessment procedures, based as they are on cultural and racial beliefs of professionals, would certainly seem to work against the children of West Indian origin.'

Further, Carrington's study (*op. cit.*) indicated that the channelling was at least partly a consequence of teachers' stereotypes of West Indians as having skills of the body rather than skills of the mind, despite 'a substantial body of research suggesting that no credence can be given to naturalistic interpretations of black sports involvement' (p. 51). Stone (1981) has similarly argued that stereotyping by teachers tends to direct Caribbean pupils away from academic pursuits, and to rationalize a 'watered down' curriculum for them. Brittan (1976) in a national study of 510 teachers in twenty-five primary and secondary schools with between 18 and 84 per cent ethnic minority pupils discovered widespread academically unfavourable stereotyping of Caribbean pupils by teachers.

Related to this, Edwards (1978, 1979) found in a study of twenty-four student teachers using tape-recordings, that they reacted negatively to Creole. The student teachers, purely on the basis of the dialect spoken, judged the West Indian speakers as having the least academic potential. The language issue is a separate and central issue, but a large and complex one, and it is reviewed elsewhere in this volume (see Edwards, pp. 79–93 and Linguistic Minorities Project, pp. 95–116). It may be, however, that what matters most here is not the language Caribbean pupils speak, but the misconceptions and stereotypes held about it by teachers — and others.

It is, indeed, not only among teachers that stereotypes of Caribbeans seem common. Besides, the issue is not one merely of stereotyping, but, more generally, of thinking, perceiving, feeling, judging, evaluating, rationalizing and acting in terms of a racist frame of reference (see Figueroa, 1983). Figueroa (1974, 1976) found evidence of such a frame of reference including negative stereotypes of West Indians, among white British pupils, and this, too, could conceivably have adverse effects on the school careers of Caribbean pupils. Similarly, Edwards (1978, 1979) in a limited but interesting study found negative attitudes towards West Indian Creole among white British pupils. Furthermore, Figueroa and Swart (1982) have found in their small-scale case study that white British pupils tended to see their West Indian peers as a good laugh, good dancers, fun-loving, having a sense of humour and the like, rather than as academic. Also, 'name calling' was common among the pupils in the school, taking place even during class.

The very ethos and curriculum of a school might have a covertly racist or culturally biased dimension, and as a result tend not to work in the best interests of black pupils. Figueroa and Swart (1982) found in, admittedly, a limited study that the teachers tended to conceptualize the 'ideal pupil' as a white, Anglo-Saxon Protestant even though the majority of the pupils in the research school consisted of Asians, Caribbeans and other ethnic minorities. They further found that very little had been done to modify the school's essentially ethnocentric curriculum.

Another factor which might help to account for some of the apparent differences in the situation of Caribbean and other ethnic minority pupils, apart from the differences in stereotyping touched on earlier, might be a differential allocation of resources (see, for instance, Bagley 1982, variables 857 and 853). Thus, much has been done about English as a second language for Asians, but very little about Standard British English where this might be helpful for Caribbean pupils (see Townsend, 1971; Little and Willey, 1981). Again, although some (limited) attention has been given to Asian mother tongue languages, even less has been given to Creole or British Black English. Referring to Nandy (1981), M. Taylor (1981, p. 234) has reported that black studies have not much affected practice. That Caribbean pupils have received comparatively little attention in practice where issues of language and culture are concerned is perhaps not surprising, since differences in these respects from the majority in the UK are perhaps less clearcut, less simple and probably less well understood and more negatively stereotyped in their case than in that of other ethnic minority groups.

Conclusion

In conclusion, although some Asians and some Caribbeans are doing well within the British educational system, overall they appear (and particularly the Caribbeans to be in an unequal position in the system. It seems to be failing them insofar as it does not seem to be very successful in fulfilling its educational task in their respect. This state of affairs is often conceptualized in terms of ethnic minority, especially Caribbean, 'underachievement'. Explanations are produced in terms of the supposed individual and group characteristics of these pupils. In particular, supposed deficiencies in or problems with the character, personality, self-concept, ability, language, culture, family organization, social background and the like in the case of the Caribbean pupils are blamed. This paper points instead to the need to investigate the structures, forces and processes within the educational system which might result in or at least do not seem so far to have been able to change this state of affairs. Much more concerted research into these complex issues is needed.

References

BAGLEY, C. (1971) 'A comparative study of social environment and intelligence in West Indian and English children in London', *Social and Economic Studies*, 20, 4, December, pp. 420–30.

BAGLEY, C. (1975) 'On the intellectual equality of races', in VERMA, G.K. and BAGLEY, C. (Eds), *Race and Education Across Cultures*, Heinemann, London.

BAGLEY, C. (1982) 'Achievement, behaviour disorder and social circumstances in West Indian children and other ethnic groups', in VERMA, G.K. and BAGLEY, C. (Eds), *Self-concept, Achievement and Multicultural Education*, London, Macmillan.

BAGLEY, C. and VERMA, G. (1972) 'Some effects of teaching designed to promote understanding of racial issues in adolescence', *Journal of Moral Education*, 1, 3, pp. 231–8.

BARNES, J. (Ed.) (1975) *Educational Priority: Curriculum Innovation in EPAs*, Vol. 3, London, HMSO.

BRITTAN, E. (1976) 'Multiracial education 2. Teacher opinion on aspects of school life. Part 2: Pupils and teachers', *Educational Research*, 18, 3, pp. 182–91.

CARRINGTON, B. (1983) 'Sport as a side-track: An analysis of West Indian involvement in extra-curricular sport', in BARTON, L. and WALKER, S. (Eds), *Race, Class and Education*, London, Croom Helm.

COARD, B. (1971) *How the West Indian Child is Made Educationally Sub-Normal in the British School System*, London, New Beacon Books.

COMMISSION FOR RACIAL EQUALITY (1978) *Ethnic Minorities in Britain: Statistical Background*, London, CRE.

CRAFT, M. (Ed.) (1981) *Teaching in a Multicultural Society: The Task for Teacher Education*, Lewes, Falmer Press.

CRAFT, M. and CRAFT, A. (1983) 'The participation of ethnic minority pupils in further and higher education', *Educational Research*, 25, 1, February, pp. 10–19.

DAVIE, R. *et al.* (1972) *From Birth to Seven*, London, Longman.

DEPARTMENT OF EDUCATION AND SCIENCE (1981) *West Indian Children in Our Schools*, ('Rampton Report'), London, HMSO.

DRIVER, G. (1980) *Beyond Underachievement: Case Studies of English, West Indian and Asian School-Leavers at 16 Plus*, London, Commission for Racial Equality.

EDWARDS, V.K. (1978) 'Language, attitudes and underperformance in West Indian children', *Educational Review*, 30, 1, pp. 51–8.

EDWARDS, V.K. (1979) *The West Indian Language Issue in British Schools*, London, Routledge and Kegan Paul.

EGGLESTON, S.J. *et al.* (1981) *In-service Teacher Education in a Multiracial Society*, Keele, University of Keele.

FETHNEY, V. (1973) 'Our ESN children', *Race Today*, 5, 4, pp. 109–15.

FIGUEROA, P.M.E. (1974) *West Indian School-Leavers in London: A Sociological Study in Ten Schools in a London Borough, 1966–1967*, unpublished PhD thesis, London School of Economics, University of London.

FIGUEROA, P.M.E. (1976) 'The employment prospects of West Indian school-leavers in London, England', *Social and Economic Studies*, 25, 3, September, pp. 216–33.

FIGUEROA, P.M.E. (1981) 'Race relations and cultural differences: Some ideas on a racist frame of reference', in VERMA, G.K. and BAGLEY, C. (Eds), *Race, Relations and Cultural Differences*, London, Croam Helm.

FIGUEROA, P.M.E. and SWART, L.T. (1982) *Poor Achievers and High Achievers among Ethnic Minority Pupils*, Report to the Commission for Racial Equality.

HALSEY, A. (1972) *Educational Priority: EPA Problems and Policies*, Vol. 1, London, HMSO.

HOUGHTON, V.P. (1966) 'Intelligence testing of West Indian and English children', *Race*, 8, pp. 147–56.

HOUSE OF COMMONS HOME AFFAIRS COMMITTEE (1981) *Racial Disadvantage*, Vol. 1, London, HMSO.

INNER LONDON EDUCATION AUTHORITY (1967) *Immigrant Children in ESN Schools: Survey Report*, London, ILEA Research and Statistics

Group, November.

INNER LONDON EDUCATION AUTHORITY (1968a) *The Education of Immigrant Pupils in Primary Schools*, Report 959, London, ILEA, February.

INNER LONDON EDUCATION AUTHORITY (1968b) *The Education of Immigrant Pupils in Special Schools for ESN Children*, Report 657, London, ILEA, September.

KAMIN, L.J. (1977) *The Science and Politics of I.Q.*, Harmondsworth, Penguin.

KARIER, C. (1976) 'Testing for order in the corporate liberal state', in DALE, R. *et al.* (Eds), *Schooling and Capitalism*, London, Routledge and Kegan Paul.

LASHLEY, H. (1979) 'Examinations and the multicultural society', *Secondary Education Journal*, 9, 2.

LITTLE, A. (1975) 'The educational achievement of ethnic minority children in London schools', in VERMA, G.K. and BAGLEY, C. (Eds), *Race and Education across Cultures*, London, Heinemann.

LITTLE, A. and WILLEY, R. (1981) *Multi-ethnic Education: The Way Forward*, London, Schools Council.

LITTLE, A. *et al.* (1968), 'The education of immigrant pupils in Inner London primary schools', *Race*, 9, 4, April.

MABEY, C. (1981) 'Black British literacy: A study of reading attainment of London black children from 8 to 15 years', *Educational Research*, 23, 2, pp. 83–95.

NANDY, D. (1981) *A Review and Assessment of Black Studies in London Schools*, SSRC report lodged with the British Library Lending Division.

OMAR, (1971) 'ESN children — labelled for life', *Race Today*, 3, 1, January, p. 2.

PAYNE, J. (1974) *Educational Priority: EPA Surveys and Statistics*, Vol. 2, London, HMSO.

REX, J. and TOMLINSON, S. (1979) (with the assistance of DAVID HEARNDEN and PETER RATCLIFFE), *Colonial Immigrants in a British City: A Class Analysis*, London, Routledge and Kegan Paul.

RUTTER, M. (1982) 'Growing up in Inner London: Problems and accomplishments', Inner City Lecture, London, IBM/North Westminster, 4 October.

SCHOOLS COUNCIL (1981), *Examining in a Multi-cultural Society*, a report of a conference held on 25 September, London, Schools Council.

STONE, M. (1981) *The Education of the Black Child in Britain: The Myth of Multiracial Education*, Glasgow, Fontana.

STONES, E. (1979) 'The colour of conceptual learning', in VERMA, G.K. and BAGLEY, C. (Eds), *Race, Education and Identity*, London, Macmillan.

TAYLOR, F. (1974) *Race, School and Community: A Study of Research and Literature*, Slough, NFER.

TAYLOR, M.J. (1981) *Caught Between: A Review of Research into the Education of Pupils of West Indian Origin*, Windsor, NFER.

TOMLINSON, S. (1980) 'The educational performance of ethnic minority children', *New Community*, 8, 3, Winter, pp. 213–34.

TOMLINSON, S. (1982) *A Sociology of Special Education*, London, Routledge and Kegan Paul.

TOWNSEND, H.E.R. (1971) *Immigrant Pupils in England: The L.E.A. Response*, Slough, NFER.

TOWNSEND, H.E.R. and BRITTAN, E.M. (1972) *Organization in Multi-Racial Schools*, Slough, NFER.

VERMA, G.K. and MALLICK, K. (1982) 'Tests and testing in a multiethnic society', in VERMA, G.K. and BAGLEY, C. (Eds), *Self-concept, Achievement and Multicultural Education*, London, Macmillan.

VERNON, P.E. (1969) *Intelligence and Cultural Environment*, London, Methuen.

VIDA, L. and FIGUEROA, P.M.E. (1983) *Examinations in a Multicultural Society: SREB Mode 1 CSE History*, University of Southampton, Department of Education, report prepared for the SREB.

WILES, S. (1968) 'Children from overseas', *Institute of Race Relations News Letter*, February/June.

YULE, W. *et al.* (1975) 'Children of West Indian immigrants — II, intellectual performance and reading attainment', *Journal of Child Psychology and Psychiatry*, 16, 1, pp. 1–17.

Home, School and Community

Sally Tomlinson

Teachers' perceptions of ethnic minority parents, and minority parents' expectations of schools are closely examined in this chapter which identifies considerable scope for improvement but some grounds for optimism.

The successful education of minority pupils depends a great deal on cooperation, communication and mutual understanding between parents and teachers — on what are termed 'good home-school relations'. Indeed, home, school and community relations have emerged as a crucial area which must be improved if minority pupils are to be offered a fair and equal education alongside their indigenous peers. It is an area in which conflicts and misunderstandings were bound to arise. Parents who were immigrants into Britain and were educated in colonial education systems had high expectations of the education system their children were entering, but lacked information and knowledge about its workings. Little provision was made until very recently, to equip teachers with any real understanding of the home and cultural backgrounds of minority pupils, or the need of their parents for help in finding their way around an unfamiliar education system. Majority society parents were often hostile to the presence of minority pupils in what they regarded as 'their' schools, and minority home-school encounters have always taken place within a society marked by racial hostility and intercultural suspicion, rather than by harmony.

However, there are no easy answers to problems and tensions arising between home and school in a multicultural society. 'Improved home-school relations' is an often-repeated rhetorical phrase, but in fact minority home-school contact is the point at which basic values can clash and seemingly irreconcilable interests present themselves.

This chapter notes the difficulty of defining 'good' home-school relations, and documents some of the dissatisfactions which minority parents are currently expressing. Minority parents' views of schools and teachers' views of minority parents and pupils are reviewed, and the mismatch of expectations between parental and community desires and teachers' offerings is discussed. The chapter then examines contact and communication with minority homes, and suggests some policies to improve home, school and community relations.

Home-School Relations

Home-school relations have never figured as a priority in education, and there is actually very little known about the purpose and effectiveness of home-school contact in general. Historically, much of the available information suggests that 'normal' home-school relations have been marked by tensions and misunderstandings and sometimes by direct conflict (Grace, 1978). As Waller wrote in his classic study of teaching (1932), 'parents and teachers usually live in conditions of mutual mistrust and enmity.' However, major efforts have been made in Britain, particularly over the past fifteen years, to improve home-school relations and to increase parental participation and involvement in the process of education. There is no general definition as to what constitutes 'good' home-school relations. Some schools may regard an absence of overt conflict and complaint as constituting good relations; others may seek the active support and involvement of as many parents as possible in school affairs before they are satisfied with their home-school relations.

Much of the literature on home and school, indicates that parental satisfaction with school and school satisfaction with home depend on children's progress and achievement. Good home-school relations are regarded by most teachers and parents as a means to the end of improving pupil attainment. Literature discussing the relationship between school achievement and home factors has tended to place some parents — particularly manual working-class parents — in an invidious position. Numerous studies have testified to the differences in achievement between the social classes; the influence of the 'good home' has been extensively documented, (Douglas, 1964, Craft, 1970); the supposed linguistic deficiencies of the working-class have attained folk-lore status (Bernstein, 1971); and compensatory education for 'the disadvantaged' has usually included attempts to 'improve' homes and parents. The Plowden Report (DES, 1967) has been a significant influence on teachers' views of homes for the past fifteen years. Plowden stressed that favourable parental attitudes towards, and interest in, education, were factors which strongly influenced children's school achievement. However, the report also stressed that parental interest did depend on the levels of knowledge parents held about education. In the 1960s levels of knowledge appeared to be low, and things may not have changed much during the 1970s. Schools and teachers do not seem to be very good at informing parents about the educational process, and find the idea of 'parents as partners' difficult to come to terms with.

The stereotyped dichotomy of the good middle-class home and the ineffective working-class home may have led many teachers to underestimate the ambitions of working-class parents to see their children succeed in education, and it may also have affected their views of minority pupils. It was unfortunate, in many ways, that the children of ethnic minority parents were entering British schools at a time when models of disadvantage and deprivation were so popular. Many teachers argued, and some still argue, that all inner city children, whether white indigenous or minority group, are equally disadvantaged. This is a simplistic view with which many minority parents disagree, and some schools are now beginning to see was mistaken.

Home-school contacts and communications have, however, improved enormously since the Plowden Committee recommended that all schools should develop special programmes for contact, including pre-school contact. Many schools have sought to involve parents much more deliberately, and the Educational Priority Area action-research teams, set up in the early 1970s, pioneered some novel forms of home-school contacts and parental education (Halsey, 1972; Smith, 1974). Written reports, increasingly seen to be an unsatisfactory area of contact, are currently being studied at the National Foundation for Educational Research; and the expansion of school support services and home-school liaison workers over the past ten years has provided contact and communication with homes. Professionals engaged in home-school liaison go under a variety of labels: home-school liaison teachers, cultural liaison teachers, community education teachers, teacher social workers, educational home visitors, youth and community workers and educational welfare officers. The status of these professionals is ambiguous, and all of them face problems of professional recognition by home, school and community.

A further advance in home-school communication is the widespread discussion of parental rights and responsibilities, which is part of a general trend towards greater accountability in education. The increased participation by parents on school management and governing bodies, following the recommendations of the Taylor Report (1977) has meant that parental participation in decision-making processes about school has, to some extent, been increased.

Home, School and Minority Parents

Despite improvements in home-school contacts, minority home-school and community relations are, in the early 1980s, in a critical phase. There is a crisis of confidence between minority homes and schools which takes the form of a questioning of the ability of schools to educate minority pupils in accordance with principles of equal opportunity and racial justice, and a questioning of the willingness of schools to genuinely accept cultural differences. There is mounting evidence to suggest that minority parents expect a good deal from the education system — far more, in many cases, than white parents. Parents of West Indian origin, in particular, are now more vocal in expressing their dissatisfactions with schools. The Rampton Committee wrote that a wide gulf in trust and understanding appeared to be growing between school and home; 'parents appear to be losing confidence in what schools are teaching their children, and schools seem to be having limited success in explaining their aims and practices' (DES, 1981, p. 41).

Minority parents have become increasingly anxious that schools are not equipping their children with the skills and credentials to compete for jobs with white pupils. These anxieties have been intensified as the economic recession has deepened, unemployment has escalated, and more qualifications are being demanded of school-leavers to compete in a shrinking job market or to go on to higher education. The issue of achievement has become a dominant concern, particularly for the West Indian community, and many parents are less willing to accept that home and family factors are primarily responsible for their children's poor school progress. Some black parents have lost faith in the ability of schools to improve things for their children; a black parent-governor recently asserted, 'we believe black underachievement can only be analysed and corrected by blacks themselves' (Neil, 1982), and there has been a sustained growth of black supplementary schools. Indeed, there has been sufficient criticism of schools, and enough initiatives taken by black educationalists, teachers and community workers to be able to speak of a Black Education movement in Britain. The participants in this movement are united by a belief that schools designed for white majority society pupils cannot offer equal opportunities to non-white children, unless they change considerably. The black parents' education movement has, over the past fifteen years, taken the form of diverse parental and community groups which have campaigned against the overrepresentation of black pupils in ESN-M schools, and disruptive units (Tomlinson, 1982; Francis, 1979), and have organized additional and supplementary education (Chevannes, 1979; Clark, 1981). Haringey Black Pressure Group on education has gone so far as to send letters to Haringey headteachers, suggesting that they have failed to provide efficient education for black pupils (see Venning, 1983).

Minority parents are also increasingly expressing their desires that cultural diversity be genuinely respected and minority cultures taken seriously in schools. Muslim parents, in particular, are increasingly in conflict with a secularized co-educational Western system, and have become more assertive of their own community needs. There is much scope for misunderstanding here, as Islamic education is based on quite different values and principles to those of English education. Muslim parents question the materialist and competitive basis of English education, the education of girls, the predominance of Christian influence, and the separation of education from other aspects of life. These issues are allied with a major anxiety of many Muslim parents — that their British-born children will move away from their faith, culture and influence. The union of Muslim organizations wrote in 1975 that 'most Muslims acknowledge that Britain is a fair place to live, . . . but it is hard to judge how possible it is to live as a Muslim in British society as a whole' (UMO, 1975, p. 10). Muslim organizations in Britain have spent some twenty years persuading schools to recognize the validity of at least some Islamic ideas in education, but many schools have been unresponsive and have found great difficulty in reconciling Muslim and English values. It is only recently that some LEAs have begun to make genuine efforts to accommodate some Muslim needs and desires (see Bradford City Council, 1982).

The crisis of confidence expressed by the black education movement and Muslim anxieties that schools will not accept cultural and religious differences are illustrations of some of the difficulties to be faced when attempts are made to put into practice exhortations for closer contact and understanding between schools and minority homes. Such exhortations have been made by various committees and commissions over the past fifteen years, for example, the Select Committee on race and immigration (1973), the DES, (1974, 1977), the Commission for Racial Equality (1978), the Home Affairs Committee (House of Commons, 1981), and the Rampton Committee (DES, 1981).

Minority Parents' Views of Education

Minority parents' views of education in Britain are influenced by their own colonial and cultural backgrounds, and by the high expectations of education nurtured in their country of origin. As the organization of Asian and African women put it: 'the dream of a good education for their children has always had a particular significance for black people ... the old colonialist equation of "education equals power" explains why so many black parents passionately wanted for their children the education they never had' (O.W.A.A.D., 1979).

Parental views are also affected by levels of education, social class, and knowledge and experience of schools and teachers in Britain. It is important to note, however, that although most minority parents in Britain are, in crude socioeconomic terms, 'working-class', their positive views and high expectations of education have always approximated more to 'middle-class' views; but they have lacked the detailed knowledge of the system which middle-class parents in Britain usually possess. In general, despite the different colonial and cultural backgrounds of minority parents in Britain, they mostly share high expectations about education and have high aspirations for their children, and they view schools as places where their children's life-chances should be enhanced. Many migrant parents, working in low-paid jobs, have felt that their lives in Britain might be justified if their children could acquire a more favourable position in society than they were able to achieve.

Despite disappointments engendered by encounters with schools and teachers, it still seems that most minority parents respect what they see as opportunities in education and expect a good deal from schools. This has been evident in research seeking the views of both Carribbean and Asian parents, although there has been considerable stereotyping of the supposed differences between these groups. Asian parents are popularly considered by teachers to be more interested in their children's education and more supportive of schools than

Carribbean parents. There is, in fact, little evidence to support this notion. What is noticeable, in studying the research, is that there is a variety of studies, often carried out by Asian researchers, which have stressed the positive interests and characteristics of Asian families (Dosanjh, 1968; Gupta, 1977; Bhatti, 1978; Ghuman, 1980; Ghuman and Gallop, 1981); while white researchers, in the search for 'explanations' of West Indian underachievement in school, have often stressed the supposed negative characteristics of Carribbean parents (Rutter *et al.*, 1974; Jackson, 1979). Carribbean parents may be, if anything, rather more likely to visit their children's schools than Asian parents (Rex and Tomlinson, 1979).

However, an important difference between the views and expectations of Asian and Carribbean parents does seem to be that from the early 1960s, Carribbean parents' expectations of school have centred on the belief that schools could offer equality of opportunity, and that this would be reflected in examination passes. Anxiety and frustration have resulted from the inability of schools to satisfy these expectations. Asian parents, expecting 'equal opportunities' have seen schools at least take their children's learning and language problems seriously, and have found their anxieties and frustrations centred more on schools' non-acceptance of cultural, religious and linguistic diversity. These differences are apparent in the research which has enquired into parental satisfaction and dissatisfaction with education.

In a study in Birmingham (Rex and Tomlinson, 1979), although over two-thirds of all minority parents expressed satisfaction with schools, Carribbean parents were more critical of what they saw as poor teaching, low standards of education, and inappropriate teaching methods. Asian (mainly Indian) parents expressed satisfaction that their children were getting regular schooling and good reports; were less likely to be critical of standards and methods; and were more interested in keeping their children in contact with religion, mother tongue and culture of origin. Carribbean parents were ambivalent about the idea of teaching 'black' cultural programmes in schools and these views have some support from black educationalists. Stone (1981) suggested that black parents want a traditional English curriculum for their children, and Woodford, a black headteacher, recently asserted that 'black parents don't want black studies or multicultural education for their children, — that is for white children; black pupils need to be good at science, history, geography, — at what society thinks of as things of worth' (Woodford, 1982).

The Birmingham study cited above indicated that all the parents were interested in their children's education, and there was little evidence of the 'parental apathy' that many teachers speak of. However, there were problems in home-school contact. Parents' evenings or open days were the times when most parents had visited the school — not the best time to establish much rapport with teachers. Caribbean and Asian parents were also more likely to be doing shift work and working longer hours than white parents, thus making it difficult for them to visit schools. It was also noticeable in this study that minority parents depended on teachers to inform them about the process of schooling, moreso than white parents, and their understanding of the curriculum and examination was limited.

Ghuman's (1980, 1981) studies of forty Jat Sikh families in the Midlands, and thirty Bengali families in Cardiff, indicated that these parents were generally satisfied with English education, valued education for its own sake, and expressed faith in teachers and their professional skills. However, issues such as single-sex schooling, dress, food, religious and mother tongue teaching were as important as issues concerning academic achievement. Muslim parents, in particular, felt their Islamic way of life was threatened if schools would not relax rules and regulations, and some parents were critical of lax discipline in schools and insufficiency of homework.

In these studies, too, parents demonstrated a lack of knowledge about school processes and curriculum. As one Bengali father said: 'because we do not know exactly what or how they teach in schools here, we cannot help our children'. More recent research[*] has indicated that, as in previous studies, minority parents do view English education as a potentially good education; but they believe strongly that it should allow for the possibility of passing examinations and acquiring skills, so that employment prospects or chances of further education are enhanced. West Indian parents also expect schools to teach their children in a disciplined and orderly manner and find it difficult to understand teachers' problems here. Asian parents expect that more of their cultural traditions will be incorporated into schools, and that schools will take more seriously the issues that concern them as parents.

---

[*] A study of twenty multiethnic schools which currently being undertaken by the Policy Studies Institute and the University of Lancaster has been examining the views of parents.

Teachers' views

A review of teachers' views and expectations of minority parents and pupils does indicate that there is a serious mismatch of expectations between what schools think they can offer minority pupils, and what minority parents want and expect. This is likely to impede the development of good home-school relations and give rise to misunderstanding. Teachers in Britain still generally lack knowledge about minority groups and hold negative and inappropriate views, particularly about Caribbean parents. Teachers generally have no clear idea of their role in a multiracial, multicultural society, and little idea of how much minority parents depend on them for information about schools and for providing their children with credentials and skills.

During the 1960s and 1970s many teachers were committed to assimilationist views and perspectives, and at the time these perspectives may have seemed appropriate. They tied in with current liberal thinking that in order to provide equal opportunities, all pupils should be treated 'the same'; and they were compatible with professional beliefs that teachers' skills should be available to all children equally. Although there is now an influential movement in education towards an acceptance of cultural diversity and alternative values, and towards combatting racism in education and society, there are undoubtedly many teachers in the 1980s still committed to assimilationist perspectives. These teachers feel genuine difficulty in responding to calls for cultural pluralism and anti-racism. A London headteacher recently argued in the columns of *The Times Educational Supplement* that 'some teachers . . . would argue that the responsibility for the adaptations and adjustments of settling in a new country lies entirely with those who have come here to settle and raise families' (Honeyford, 1982).

However, other teachers would argue that the school system also has a responsibility to adapt and change. It is not surprising, however, that some teachers have come to hold inappropriate, stereotyped or negative beliefs about minorities, and some feel threatened or defensive in their contacts with minority parents. Teachers in Britain are mainly white, middle-class and educated into what the DES (1977) has referred to as a 'curriculum appropriate to our Imperial past'. During their training they have seldom received help or encouragement to develop more positive views about minorities, or to learn skills of contact and communication with minority parents. This aspect of teacher training has never been regarded as an urgent priority, and there has never been any coordinated national policy to ensure that intending teachers received any 'multicultural' training. This lack of preparation has been deplored at length in government reports and research (DES, 1977, 1981; House of Commons, Home Affairs Committee 1981; Little and Willey, 1981). However, in the 1980s there are some signs that teacher training may be beginning to face up to 'multicultural' preparation, however fraught with difficulties.

It is certainly now possible to detail some of the inappropriate views of minority parents, pupils and communities which some teachers hold, and to consider their possible consequences. First, there is evidence of what Khan (1980) has called 'elaborate structures of myth-making'. Lacking real knowledge of the cultural backgrounds of minorities or of their lives in Britain, teachers resort to stereotypes or half-truths which may be more of a barrier to home-school understanding than admitted ignorance. Khan uses the popular stereotypes of Muslim families — 'they don't want to mix — the father won't let the mother come to school — they spend hours at the mosque — the girls have to do all the domestic work', to show that crude beliefs can actually prevent contact between home and school. Similarly crude beliefs about Caribbean parents, particularly mothers — 'they all go out to work, the children are child-minded, they have few toys or books in the home, they all believe in corporal punishment' — have probably prevented rather than assisted communication with parents.

A second inappropriate view of minorities may be teachers' popular belief that minority parents and pupils are all part of a group loosely labelled 'the disadvantaged'. The Birmingham study (Rex and Tomlinson, 1979) found that many teachers stressed material disadvantages — poor housing and environment, unskilled or unemployed parents — rather than disadvantages concerned with race, colour or migration; and that the 'disadvantaged' approach led some heads to view their schools in a social-pastoral context rather than as examination-oriented, academic places. Some teachers felt that lower standards and expectations were inevitable with a multiracial intake, and, although they tried to make schools a pleasant environment, did not expect high achievement. This, of course, was the antithesis of the expectations and understandings of minority parents as to what schools were all about. The one crucial way in which minority parents were disadvantaged in education — by not having sufficient knowledge and experience of the process — was not acknowledged by the schools in this study, nor, it seems, by other schools. Immigrant minority parents, who have needed more help than even white 'disadvantaged' parents, who at least have been through the school system, have never been the specific focus of teachers' attention.

A third, and perhaps the most extensively documented, inappropriate view held by many teachers, has been their persistent stereotyping of Caribbean parents and pupils as difficult and problematic. It has not been uncommon to hear this view expressed by teachers in 'white' schools who have never taught minority pupils. Stereotyped and negative views of West Indians have undoubtedly been translated into classroom action (Green, 1982), with effects on West Indian school performance.

It is not surprising that many teachers of pupils of West Indian origin have felt uncomfortable in discussing the low achievement of the pupils with their parents, and have preferred explanations for poor performance located in the home and family rather than in the school and the teaching.

A Mismatch of Expectations

There is undoubtedly a mismatch of expectations and basic value differences between what minority parents expect of education and what schools and teachers think they can offer. This makes good home-school relations more difficult to achieve. However, the basis for this mismatch does not necessarily lie in any deliberate obtuseness of teachers. The mismatch rests ultimately on the existing structures and functions of the education system and on its cultural content, and it may not be in the interests of school to explain to any group of parents what structural limitations there are on access to 'equal opportunities'.

Minority parents' satisfactions with the education system — 'its there for them to take advantage of' as one West Indian mother put it — rests on the post-war liberal notion that 'equal chances to be unequal' do prevail in education. But the ending of the tripartite system and moves to comprehensivization have not increased the possibility of equal opportunity for most children. The chances of children of manual working-class parentage being selected and prepared for an academically-oriented education which allows access to higher education have not improved, and most inner city schools — the ones attended by most minority pupils — are not geared to high level academic work or a technical curriculum. Many such schools are now beginning to realize that they incorporate minority pupils of all levels of ability, but they do not have the resources or the skills to develop academic abilities, and it is unclear how far new developments in technical education will affect minority pupils. Confusion and difficulties are likely to persist unless schools can openly discuss with parents the kind of education they offer.

Explanations regarding schools' levels of acceptance of cultural diversity is another area where misunderstandings may be perpetuated. The areas where Asian parents would like to see most change — in the education of girls, mother tongue teaching, religious education, and less participation in extra-curricular activities — are all areas which teachers may find difficulty in coming to terms with. The cultural content of the education system is based on particular beliefs and values which are distinctly at odds with some Asian cultural beliefs and values. This is not to deny the importance of curricular change, which will hopefully alter the ethnocentric nature of the curriculum, but it does mean that teachers will have to be very clear about the value base of their curriculum practice. A mismatch between school and community understandings of 'cultural diversity' may continue to be a source of home-school tension.

Contact and Communication

Despite problems and tensions concerning contradictory expectations of parents and teachers, there is a variety of initiatives currently being undertaken by some LEAs and schools to improve minority home-school contact and communicate more clearly with parents. It is becoming clearer that although a good deal of the improved contact is along the familiar 'Plowden' lines of parents' days and evenings, PTAs, welcoming parents in school, pre-school groups and visits and community school activity, there are also new-style links in the form of genuine discussion with community leaders and parents' representatives, debates on parental rights and duties, and the involvement of some parents, as school governors, in educational decision-making.

By 1981 some twenty-eight LEAs had appointed multicultural education advisors and were giving serious consideration to minority home-school links, and about ten LEAs were in the process of producing written policy guidelines to assist schools in their dealings with minorities. In Berkshire, for example, an advisory committee for multicultural education — chaired by the Director of Education — was set up in 1981 to debate a variety of issues concerning 'education for equality', including the question: 'what should be done to increase mutual understanding between schools and parents, and how should issues to do with equality and racism be raised and handled?' (Berkshire, 1982, p. 14). It was noteworthy that representatives from seventeen minority organizations were involved with this committee, including the Reading Asian Parents Group, the Pakistani Parents Society, the West Indian Peoples' Association, and the West Indian Womens' Circle. The committee produced a discussion leaflet, translated into three minority languages, for all schools and parents in the area, and invited views and comments.

In Bradford the LEA produced guidelines for schools setting out a policy for education in a multicultural society. The importance of home-school contacts and parental rights were the first issues raised in these guidelines. Page one noted that:

> it is important that minority parents should — as should all parents — become familiar with the nature of the schooling their children are receiving, and be enabled to discuss difficulties that this may present for them. A clash of aims in the education of the child may undermine the opportunity for the child to take full advantage of the education system (Bradford, 1982).

For most LEAs and schools who are taking minority home-school contacts seriously, the importance of actually bringing parents and teachers together to discuss educational issues and problems is certainly recognized, but there are problems with methods of implementation. While many schools recognize that there is insufficient time for educational discussion between parents and teachers, the solution of many local authorities has been to interpose an extra 'layer' of professionals in the form of liaison teachers. The idea of home-school liaison teachers dates back to a suggestion by the Plowden Committee in 1967, and during the 1970s many LEAs appointed such teachers. By 1980, some had been renamed 'cultural liaison' or 'community' teachers, and were seeking to consolidate a more autonomous professional status. Little and Willey, reporting their national survey of local education authorities in 1981, noted that while only 11 per cent of schools in the survey actually said they had home-school liaison teachers, one LEA reported appointing twenty home-school liaison officers with money from the Manpower Services Commission, and another LEA. had appointed a group of 'cultural liaison' teachers specifically to work with minority parents (Little and Willey, 1981). Little and Willey also reported that several authorities claimed to discuss educational issues with local community leaders and with local community relations committees.

Improved home-school contact and communication is thus often regarded as a matter for 'liaison' by special professionals, or by consultation with community 'leaders' — who may or may not represent a full spectrum of parental views. There is little research providing information as to how parents perceive and react to community liaison or home-school teachers. On the positive side, minority parents in particular may appreciate discussion with a 'teacher' who, not being involved in full-time teaching, actually has time to talk to parents and explain educational problems. Parents may also appreciate the use of extra professional skills in organizing pre-school groups, parents 'in the classroom', parental activities in school, language classes for Asian parents, and so on. On the negative side, however, an extra 'layer' of professionals could mean that parents see even less of the teachers who actually teach their children than before. Liaison teachers may become the professionals who deal with 'difficult' or ill-informed parents, and they may not be in a position to discuss what many parents actually want to discuss — the performance of individual children and teaching strategies to improve individual performance.

However, if 'liaison' is dispensed with and contact and communication with parents encouraged at the individual teacher level, more school time will have to be made available for such activities. The Rampton Committee suggested that a senior member of staff in all schools take on the additional task of coordinating links between the school and the community, and that 'teachers should see home-school visiting as an integral part of their pastoral responsibilities' (DES, 1981, p. 80). Taking time away from teaching activities may not, in fact, be assisting pupil achievement — the issue, as we have noted, that most concerns minority parents. There are particular problems concerning the professional definition of the teacher's role when improved contact and communication with minority homes is called for.

Improved Practice

This chapter has attempted to show that current tensions and problems between minority homes and schools are based on clashes of values and mismatches in expectations, and that there is a lack of knowledge and misunderstanding on both sides. The achievement of improved home-school relations is thus no easy task. There is, as we have noted, no general feeling that parents, particularly working-class parents, should be involved in the state education of their children to any great extent; and despite major efforts to improve practice over the past fifteen years, 'good home-school relations' are often more of a pious hope than a reality. Much of the improvement in home-school relations has been produced on an *ad hoc* basis by the initiative of individual schools and LEAs, and local authorities with large numbers of minority pupils may actually have been in the vanguard of the movement to improve home-school relations generally.

However, an important question remains as to how far policies to improve home-school relations should be specifically aimed at minority parents, and how far at all parents. Since there are no overall national home-school policies in Britain, suggestions for improved national practice must remain in the realm of speculation at the moment. However, one particular policy, adopted on a national scale for all parents, could be of particular benefit to minority parents. This is the policy suggested by McBeth to the Commission of the European Communities at a conference on the school and family in Europe (see Wilce, 1983). McBeth has suggested a 'School and Family Concordat', a contractual agreement between schools and parents, by which parental rights and duties and the duties of schools and teachers would be spelled out, so that each party would be clear about rights, responsibilities and expectations. McBeth envisages that the school and family concordat would oblige schools and teachers to cooperate with parents, and would certainly benefit minority parents by ensuring parent-teacher contact, and improving teachers' knowledge about minorities. Spelling out the duties of schools would also help minority parents and communities understand more clearly the dilemmas inherent in attempting to provide equal opportunities and opportunities for cultural diversity

There is also scope for specific policies aimed at minorities. Since minority parents expect a good deal, but lack information about the education system, community and liaison teachers could be given the specific brief of informing minority parents about the processes, possibilities and limitations of the education system. Schools with large numbers of minority parents could automatically adopt the policy of translating all home-school literature and reports, offer separate parents' meetings to different ethnic groups who may need to discuss their own problems, and have at least one minority parent-governor. Ideally, also, special pre-school education should be offered to all minority children, to prepare them for education in a system still largely designed to accommodate white majority society children.

Whatever new policies may be adopted, it is certain that unthinkingly offering more of the palliatives that have often passed for 'improved home-school contacts' will not solve the crisis of confidence between minority homes and schools. The issues at stake are the ability of schools to educate minority pupils in accordance with principles of social and racial justice — attempting to offer equal opportunities and respect cultural differences and diversity — and this demands new and more radical home-school policies than those previously offered.

References

BERKSHIRE DEPARTMENT OF EDUCATION (1982) *Education for Equality: A Paper for Discussion in Berkshire*, Advisory Committee on Multicultural Education, Reading, Berks.

BERNSTEIN, B. (1973) *Class, Codes and Control*, Vol. 1, London, Routledge and Kegan Paul.

BHATTI, F.M. (1978) 'Young Pakistanis in Britain, educational needs and problems', *New Community*, 6, 3.

BRADFORD CITY COUNCIL (1982) *Education for a Multicultural Society: Provision for Pupils of Ethnic Minorities in Schools*, Bradford.

CHEVANNES, M. (1979) 'The Black Arrow Supplementary School Project', *The Social Science Teacher*, 8, 4.

CLARK, N. (1982) 'Dachwyng Saturday School', in OHRI, A. *et al.* (Eds), *Community Work and Racism*, London, Routledge and Kegan Paul.

CRAFT, M. (Ed.) (1970) *Family, Class and Education*, London, Longman.

DEPARTMENT OF EDUCATION AND SCIENCE (1967) *Children and Their Primary Schools*, ('Plowden Report'), London, HMSO.

DEPARTMENT OF EDUCATION AND SCIENCE (1974) *Educational Disadvantage and the Needs of Immigrants*, London, HMSO.

DEPARTMENT OF EDUCATION AND SCIENCE (1977) *Education in Schools — A Consultative Document*, London, HMSO.

DEPARTMENT OF EDUCATION AND SCIENCE (1981) *West Indian Children in Our Schools*, Report of the Committee of Enquiry into the Education of Children from Ethnic Minority Groups, ('Rampton Report'), London, HMSO.

DOSANJH, J.S. (1968) 'Punjabi immigrant children — their social and emotional problems', *Education Paper No. 10*, Institute of Education, University of Nottingham.

DOUGLAS, J.W.B. (1964) *The Home and the School*, London, McGibbon and Kee.

FRANCIS, M. (1979) 'Disruptive units — labelling a new generation', *New Approaches in Multi-Racial Education*, 8, 1.

GHUMAN, P.A. (1980) 'Punjabi parents and English education', *Educational Research*, 22, 2.

GHUMAN, P.A. and GALLOP, R. (1981) 'Educational attitudes of Bengali families in Cardiff', *Journal of Multi-Cultural and Multi-Lingual Development*, 2, 2.

GRACE, G. (1978) *Education, Ideology and Social Control*, London, Routledge and Kegan Paul.

GREEN, P. (1982) *Teachers Influence on the Self-Concept of Pupils of Different Ethnic Origins*, unpublished PhD thesis, University of Durham.

GUPTA, P. (1977), 'Educational and vocational aspirations of Asian immigrants and English school-leavers', *British Journal of Sociology*.

HALSEY, A.H. (1972), *Educational Priority, EPA Policies and Problems*, London, HMSO.

HONEYFORD, R. (1982) 'Multi-racial myths', *The Times Educational Supplement*, 19 November 1982.

HOUSE OF COMMONS, HOME AFFAIRS COMMITTEE (1981) *Racial Disadvantage*, London, HMSO.

JACKSON, M. and JACKSON, S. (1979) *Child Minder*, London, Routledge and Kegan Paul.

LITTLE, A. and WILLEY, R. (1981) *Multi-Ethnic Education — the Way Forward*, London, Schools Council.

NEIL, A. (1982) 'In loco parentis', *Issues in Race and Education*, 37, p. 6.

ORGANISATION OF WOMEN OF ASIAN AND AFRICAN DESCENT (1979) 'Black Education', *Forward*, Spring.

REX, J. and TOMLINSON, S. (1979) *Colonial Immigrants in a British City: A Class Analysis*, London, Routledge and Kegan Paul.

RUTTER, M. *et al.* (1974) 'Children of West Indian immigrants — 1. Rates of behavioural deviance and psychiatric disorder', *Journal of Child Psychology and Psychiatry*, 15.

SMITH, G. (Ed.) (1974) *Educational Priority*, Vol. 4, The West Riding Project, London, HMSO.

TOMLINSON, S. (1982) *A Sociology of Special Education*, London, Routledge and Kegan Paul.

UNION OF MUSLIM ORGANISATIONS OF THE UK AND EIRE (1975) *Islamic Education and Single-sex Schools*, London.

VENNING, P. (1983) 'Menacing warning sent to Haringey heads over exams' *The Times Educational Supplement*, 11 February 1983.

WILCE, H. (1983) 'Co-operation pledge plan drawn up for parents' *The Times Educational Supplement*, 25 March 1983.

WOODFORD, O. (1982) Interview on *Ebony*, BBC TV, 17 November 1982.

Ideologies and Multicultural Education*

Robert Jeffcoate

In this final chapter Robert Jeffcoate seeks to examine some of the explicit and hidden assumptions of contemporary commentaries on the principles and practice of education in a plural society.

Education and race relations are both contested areas of study and intervention; so it is hardly surprising that multicultural education, which straddles the two, should have become a site for ideological debate and conflict. In this chapter I want to examine the nature of that debate and that conflict, and to take a particularly critical look at those ideologies I shall call radical or Marxist. But before proceeding I should perhaps explain that I shall be using 'multicultural education' in two senses. First, as an area of study and intervention. Second, as referring to a loosely connected collection of policies frequently enjoined upon, and to some extent taken up by, central government, local authorities and schools, and which could be said to be united by two aims: the amelioration of the educational position of children from the *ethnic minorities*, and the preparation of *all pupils*, irrespective of the ethnic composition of their schools and neighbourhoods, for adulthood in a multiethnic society.

I should also explain that I am not using 'ideology' in the Marxist sense of ideas propagated to serve a particular social class or economic interest, but more broadly to denote a system of beliefs that provides

---

* This chapter is a development of material originally prepared for Open University course E354, *Ethnic Minorities and Community Relations*, which was presented to students for the first time in 1982. However, the views expressed are those of the author and not of the Open University or the course team.

the basis for analysis and directs action. For me this definition has the advantage of descriptive neutrality. It does not imply, as pejorative Marxist usage so often does, the presence of ulterior motives, sinister subterfuges and secret cabals among the ideologies under examination. Yet at the same time I shall certainly be arguing that the strength of ideological commitment in the field of multicultural education has tended to override concern for accuracy and truth, and has resulted in faulty analysis and misconceived recommendations for action.

Liberalism

Setting on one side conservative and reactionary ideologies, which are not my concern here, the debate about multicultural education (in both the senses indicated above) can, I think, be conceptualized, without too much simplification, as a contest between two competing ideologies, liberalism and radicalism, and as such forms part of a wider debate about the relationship between schools, or the education system, and society. Liberalism, the moving spirit (it might be said) behind the inception of state education in Britain in the final quarter of the nineteenth century, and predictably dominating educational theory and policy in most of the twentieth, emerged out of the confluence of three ideological tributaries. The oldest was the Romantic libertarian tradition of creativity and self-fulfilment whose source can be traced back to Rousseau; and which was to find a useful scientific ally in developmental psychology, and be most famously realized in the child-centred primary schools extolled by the Plowden Report in 1967, and 'progressive' schools in the independent sector such as A.S. Neill's Summerhill. Secondly, there was the Victorian meritocratic philosophy memorably summarized by Thomas Huxley when a member of the first London School Board in 1871 — 'I conceive it to be our duty to make a ladder from the gutter to the university along which any child may climb' — and transformed ninety years later, with the support of Conservative as well as of Labour and Liberal politicians, into positive discrimination measures to promote equal opportunity for the socially disadvantaged. Finally, there was the ideal of a democratic education, or of education for adulthood in a Parliamentary democracy, which owed a particular debt to John Dewey and the history of the American 'common' school, and spoke of maximizing society's talents and fostering rationality, considerateness and empathy. This led eventually to comprehensivization, the 'community' school, and experiments in more democratic forms of government and control along the lines pioneered by Neill at Summerhill.

Liberalism has been equally dominant among schoolteachers, or rather among that minority of a mainly conservative profession who are persuaded of the need for change, and especially in the more optimistic economic and social climate that prevailed from, say, the Labour victory in 1945 to the Labour defeat in 1970. Comprehensivization and positive discrimination have been complemented in the classroom by experiments with mixed ability grouping, integrated curricula, and collaborative and less formal methods of teaching and learning. Multicultural education, in the normative sense of a set of preferred policies, is an unmistakeable product of the liberal ideology in its 1960s heyday. The first three official pronouncements on the subject — Ministry of Education Pamphlet 43, *English for Immigrants* (1963), the second report of the Commonwealth Immigrants Advisory Council (1964), and Circular 7/65 (1965) — and the earliest policy initiatives, which, with the exception of dispersal (never pursued with enthusiasm and soon abandoned), still provide the basis for the orthodox view on multicultural education, were all imbued with the spirit of one or more of the liberal traditions I have identified.

Steps undertaken by central and local government for the recruitment of extra staff and the provision of extra funds to cater for the linguistic and cultural needs of pupils from the ethnic minorities belonged within the tradition of discriminating positively to secure equal opportunities for the socially disadvantaged. The creed of integrationism — the multiracial school as a microcosm of a harmonious multiracial society in which children from different ethnic backgrounds work and play together as equals — was a specific manifestation of a more general belief, prominent in the 1960s, in the power of a genuinely 'common' school, admitting all children from a given catchment area regardless of ability, class, sex, religion or race; and adapting curricular and other policies accordingly, to dispel prejudice, foster rationality and create social cohesion. While the celebration of the ethnic transformation of Britain as a resource for curriculum enrichment (as applicable, argued those official pronouncements of the early 1960s, to schools unaffected by the transformation directly as dispelling prejudice and fostering rationality), demonstrated the strength of the hedonistic view of education — school as a place to enjoy oneself — that inspired the tradition stretching from Rousseau to Neill. The dominance of liberalism in the field of multicultural education over the past twenty years has

undoubtedly reflected the ideology's overall dominance in educational debate and decision-making.

Radicalism

On the whole, radicals take a pretty dim view of liberalism and all its
works. They castigate it for its individualism, its naive optimism, its
lack of theoretical rigour, and its failure to confront inequality and
injustice. It is, they stress, a meritocratic creed, not an egalitarian one;
dedicated to the enhancement of individual life chances, not to the
redistribution of wealth, power or status, and as such the perfect
apologia for retaining the arrangements of a capitalist society — in
other words, an 'ideology' in the Marxist sense. Whether radicals call
themselves Marxists or not, it is the Marxist analysis of the relationship between schools and society which furnishes radicalism with
its theoretical underpinning and some of its most distinctive features.
Where liberalism is preoccupied with the *aims* of a formal system of
education, what schools can and should set out to achieve, Marxism is
preoccupied with its *function* under capitalism, what it actually does
irrespective of the aims that have been set. Where liberals quote
Thomas Huxley on equal opportunity, Marxists quote the slogans of
Victorian politicians and industrialists — 'gentling the masses',
'educating our masters' — anxious for a state system of education
which would turn out a literate electorate and a disciplined workforce.

   According to Marxist ideology, the essential function of schools
under capitalism is to reproduce its class structure and social divisions. Schools are seen to perform this task in several ways. First,
they satisfy the demands of the labour market by classifying and
selecting children for appropriate employment in an apparently
objective manner. Secondly, they reproduce the hierarchies typical of
places of work, in their patterns of authority and control; and,
thirdly, they institutionalize in curriculum choices, disciplinary measures, and overall ethos the interests and values of the middle class. In
effect, then, the Marxist ideology identifies the education system as a
vehicle of social control that, far from (as liberals mistakenly imagine)
promoting equality of opportunity, social mobility or enlightened
attitudes, both reinforces and justifies existing inequalities. It is a
decisive instrument — the key 'ideological state apparatus', in the
phrase of the French Marxist, Althusser — for maintaining the
hegemony of the middle class, and for socializing working-class

children into employment as industrial helots, 'hewers of wood and drawers of water'. As a result, schools represent an alienating experience for working-class children who underachieve academically on a massive scale, and become arenas for class conflict. Recognizing (if only partially or unconsciously) what schools are up to, and that liberalism's noble aims do not apply to them, working-class children resist, through truancy, apathy or indiscipline.

Although Marxism has never boasted a large following in Britain (attributable to, as much as anything, the penchant of Marxist writers for incomprehensible prose — an oddity in an ideology supposedly speaking to and on behalf of the working class), it has enjoyed some success in intellectual circles, particularly sociological ones, since the insurrectionary events in European cities in the late 1960s. During the depressing atmosphere of the 1970s, the decade of deepening economic recession, falling school rolls, cuts in public expenditure, teacher and youth unemployment, and public concern over standards, discipline and truancy, it forged somewhat unlikely alliances with American deschoolers and European phenomenologists (notably in critical analysis of the school's 'hidden' curriculum); and many of its tenets, and much of its obscure vocabulary, passed into the conventional wisdom of initial and in-service teacher education. Bowles and Gintis's *Schooling in Capitalist America*, published in this country in 1976 as a set book for the influential Open University course *Schooling and Society* (the target, along with other OU courses, for accusations of Marxist bias from conservative educationists), almost achieved the status of a sacred text. It would be no exaggeration to say that during this period Marxism replaced liberalism as the dominant ideology of educational theory and analysis; but not, of course, of educational policy, where the liberal doctrine of gradual and piecemeal reform (an apposed to radical restructuring) continued, and continues, to hold sway; nor, indeed, among forward-looking school teachers of whom radicals and Marxists, whatever publicity or notoriety they may have attracted, constitute only a small minority.

Ideological Variations

My portraits of liberalism and radicalism run the risk, perhaps, of suggesting that the two ideologies are discrete monolithic entities free from internal variation and dispute, whereas in fact precisely the opposite is the case. There are tensions within liberalism — between moralists and hedonists, meritocrats and progressivists, and utilitarians and utopians — and Marxism is well-known for its internecine factionalism, a legacy of the fact that Marx wrote so much and left his *magnum opus* incomplete. A particular focus for debate among Marxists has been the relationship between 'base' and 'superstructure'; that is to say, between the economic structure of a society (or, in Marxist language, the material conditions of production) and its culture (its institutions, the arts, the world of ideas). One of Marx's most famous dicta runs: 'It is not the consciousness of men that determines their social being, but, on the contrary, their social being that determines their consciousness.' From which it might be reasonable to infer that he at any rate had a fairly uncomplicated view of the relationship. However, this has not prevented his followers dividing into those, on the one hand, who attach primacy to 'base' and relegate the ingredients of the 'superstructure' to the role of functions or products of economic exigencies (in other words, who agree with the dictum as I read it); and those on the other hand, who, deriving their inspiration from Marx's early writings and the work of the Italian Marxist Gramsci, argue in favour of a dialectical relationship between 'base' and 'superstructure' and the relative autonomy of the latter.

In educational terms this division corresponds to the difference between believing that, without the socialist transformation of society, schools and teachers (notwithstanding the considerable independence ostensibly bestowed upon them by a decentralized system of education) can only ever serve to reproduce capitalism's inequalities and injustices, and believing that, far from being the puppets of forces beyond their control, they actually have an important part to play in bringing that transformation about. What that might mean in practice — how Lenin's question: 'What is to be done?' should be answered in relation to education — has produced a further round of dissension among Marxists, or at any rate among Marxists inclining towards a dialectical rather than a deterministic interpretation of the relationship between 'base' and 'superstructure'. Gramsci himself, taking what now seems a rather conservative line, insisted that, if the bourgeois hegemony was to be replaced by a proletarian one, the working class must first acquire mastery over the cultural 'baggage' of necessary knowledge and skills represented by the established curriculum (Entwistle, 1979). Later Marxist educationists have emphasized either the development in children of a critical socialist consciousness (exposing capitalism's inherent iniquities and contradictions), or else moulding the working-class counter-cultures generated by the alienating experience of school into a revolutionary force. Liberal commentators have been quick to point out that once in operation socialist education systems are invariably indoctrinatory in character — the model for emulation suspiciously resembling the recitation of a religious catechism.

At this juncture it is important to recognize the areas of overlap, the common ground, shared or contested by liberalism and radicalism. Just as liberals are by no means all unimpressed or uninfluenced by Marxist analysis, so when it comes to classroom practice radical teachers in Britain are more than likely to resort to the Liberal repertoire of child-centred techniques, albeit claiming (and with good reason) that several of them — collaborative learning, say, or team teaching — owe more to the radical principles of cooperation and solidarity than to anything in the liberal tradition. Indeed, I think it is probably true to say that many forward-looking teachers remain ideologically ambivalent, seduced by Marxist analysis yet dedicated to liberal aims. Nonetheless, there can be little question of the fundamental divorce between the two ideologies. In his recent book on the comprehensive school, David Hargreaves has summarized the differences at the pedagogic level as follows:

> The 'liberal' teacher interprets his task as the preparation of self-confident autonomous adults; the 'radical' teacher interprets his task as, in addition, the provision of the pupil with an insight into inequalities and injustices which prevail in contemporary British society.... Pupils are to be prepared not with the qualities of utopia, to ensure its emergence, as in the case of the progressive, but with the knowledge and skills to fight capitalism, to ensure its defeat, for that is the first and primary step in the creation of the utopia. (Hargreaves, 1982, pp. 93–4, 96).

The divorce might be represented at a more general level by suggesting that liberals would have been happier if the Victorian sage with the greatest influence on the twentieth century had been John Stuart Mill, not Karl Marx.

Race and Racism

Of special significance for the debate about multicultural education are the disagreements between Marxists, and between Marxists and liberals, over race and racism. Marxist wrangling on this topic has followed a more than usually tortuous path; so it is useful to have John Gabriel and Gideon Ben-Tovim's article, 'Marxism and the concept of racism' (published in 1978), available as a guide through some of the denser thickets of discourse. From their exegesis it is clear that what unites Marxists is the conviction that racism is specific to capitalism. Effectively, they reduce it to: the transatlantic slave trade and European colonialism; the ideologies developed to justify them; and those forms of racial exploitation and injustice bequeathed to a post-emancipation, post-colonial world which survive because they continue to fulfil economic and/or political functions. What divides Marxists is the precise nature of the relationship between racist beliefs and racialist practices, and the demands of a capitalist economy; in other words, it is a particular example of the more general dissension over the relationship between 'base' and 'superstructure.'

Two points are worth stressing about the Marxist position. First of all, the restriction of racism to Western capitalism seems perversely at variance with commonsense usage. As Gabriel and Ben-Tovim point out, there is little to distinguish the content of the racism which evolved in conjunction with the inauguration of the transatlantic slave trade and European colonial expansion, from the content of pre-capitalist modes of racial antagonism and discrimination, or indeed of contemporary manifestations in socialist countries which Marxists prefer to conceptualize as ethnocentricism. For example, *The Guardian* for 10 July 1979 carried a news story, headlined 'Foreign students injured in China race riot', which described how three days of fighting between Chinese and black students at Shanghai's Textile Institute ended with twelve foreigners needing hospital treatment; and also how, in a separate incident at the same time, an African student was arrested after a fight had erupted when he danced with a Chinese girl in a city park. To a non-Marxist, antagonism and violence directed by Chinese against Africans (accompanied, incidentally, in the first episode by the insult 'black devils') are as much displays of racism as antagonism and violence directed by whites against Bangladeshis in London's East End. Confining racism to white oppression of blacks or, in a separate but related context, reducing it to the status of an adjunct of Fascism, is really to be guilty of what Karl Popper has called 'essentialism', whereby a word is defined not, as in a dictionary, according to its actual use, but by reference to some supposed 'real' or 'true' meaning which exists 'out there', independent of, and superior to, popular usage (Popper, 1976, pp. 17–31). A crude form of this fallacy, current in radical circles in recent years, is the formula, 'racism equals prejudice plus power', the burden of which seems to be that in Britain only whites can ever be racist.

Paradoxically — and this is the second main point I want to make about the Marxist position — the Marxist predilection for a restricted definition of racism has been complemented by a pronounced tendency to exaggerate its incidence and prevalence. Whereas liberals, who by and large go along with a commonsensical dictionary definition, acknowledge racism's existence only when there is hard evidence (as in the case of racial discrimination in employment, or racially motivated attacks on ethnic minorities), radicals decry its influence in every nook and cranny, place cynical constructions upon seemingly benevolent acts in order to unearth racist motives, and deal in sweeping and unfalsifiable assertions about Britain being an inherently, endemically and (even occasionally) irreversibly racist society. A good example of this tendency is the way radicals have exploited the concept of 'institutional' racism. Lord Scarman, an intelligent outsider and a liberal by disposition, was evidently puzzled by the way the allegation of institutional racism kept cropping up in the evidence he received on the causes of the Brixton riots of 1981. To him, and many liberals, an institutionally racist society means one which, in the words of his Report, 'knowingly, as a matter of policy, discriminates' against certain ethnic groups. On the basis of this definition, South Africa is such a society, and slavery in the Caribbean, segregation in the southern United States, and discrimination in Britain's colonies could all be cited as historical examples of institutional racism elsewhere. But Lord Scarman was quite adamant that institutional racism in this sense does not exist in Britain today (Home Office, 1981). Most liberals would, I think, be inclined to agree with him, while making an exception of immigration control and the 1981 British Nationality Act, since their combined, if unstated, object is to limit the number of British citizens who are not white.

Radicals, however, have extended the meaning of institutional racism to make it virtually synonymous with what in the 1976 Race Relations Act is called 'indirect discrimination'. Frequently-quoted instances in the field of education are the over representation of West Indian children in disruptive units, suspensions, bottom and remedial streams, and in special schools for the maladjusted and the educationally subnormal; the use of standardized assessment tests which are neither culture-fair nor culture-free; curricula and examination syllabuses which take no account of cultural diversity; and arrangements for religious assembly, girls' PE and school dinners which ignore the requirements of ethnic minorities. To the extent that these phenomena still disfigure the British education system they are certainly to be deplored; only adherents of conservative or reaction-ary ideologies could afford to feel defensive about them. Yet labelling them instances of institutional racism is, from the standpoint of the commonsense use of racism, to beg the question of their aetiology, and to take for granted what has still to be demonstrated — namely, that it is to be located in the prevalence of racist beliefs among those responsible. In sum, then, to suit its ideological purposes Marxist usage both denies the existence of racism when most other people find it present, and finds it present when most other people remain agnostic.

Race, Class, and Anti-Racism

Two other aspects of Marxist dissension over racism discussed by Gabriel and Ben-Tovim which have relevance for the debate about multicultural education are the disagreements over race and class, and over anti-racist policy and strategy. The problem liberals have in following the Marxist argument about race and class is, once again, mainly a matter of semantics. Marx's dualist model of social class, distinguishing only bourgeoisie and proletariat or the ownership and non-ownership of the means of production, seems, whatever merits it may have had in the Victorian era, strangely dated and barely compatible with the model normally used by social scientists today — the Registrar General's fivefold classification of employment statuses or some version of it. While 'races', in Gabriel and Ben-Tovim's words, 'are not strictly real economic categories, but are rather false ideological representations which are the product of *myths* about human classification.' Perhaps as a result of their ideological obsession with black-white relations, Marxists (but not only Marxists) have been inclined to confuse 'race' with colour; very largely ignoring the experience and situation of British ethnic minor-ities (the Irish, Jews, gypsies, Italians, Chinese) who are not usually thought of as 'black', but have certainly been treated or regarded as identifiable 'races'.

The central line of Marxist argument has been about precisely how stratification by class and stratification by race intersect and interact, if at all; or, to put it another way, about whether race is a subset of class, whether ethnic minorities, or blacks, can be characte-rized as a subproletariat or at least some kind of class fraction. Everyday observation and the available empirical evidence (from national censuses, PEP research, the National Dwelling and Household Survey and local studies) suggest that they cannot; or rather that there is such considerable variation between the positions of different ethnic minorities — between, say, that of the gypsies (whose children were described by the Plowden Report in 1967 as 'probably the most severely deprived' in the country) and that of the Jews (with forty-six Members of Parliament in 1974) — as to disqualify all attempts at a generalized characterization. Even within the category 'blacks' there is a marked difference between the position of Pakistanis and Bangladeshis, whose employment profile is skewed towards disadvantage in several key aspects, and that of South Asians born in India and East Africa, whose employment profile corresponds closely to that for the working population as a whole. Needless to add, these facts have not prevented Marxists, never noted for their respect for empirical data, from pursuing their essentially theoretical discussions about whether ethnic minorities or blacks can or cannot be conceptualized as an underclass.

Similarly, the ideological postures underlying these same discussions have had more bearing on the attitudes adopted by Marxists towards the second topic for debate — choice of anti-racist policy and strategy — than any *facts* that might be to hand. Gabriel and Ben-Tovim's analysis draws a broad line between Marxists (mostly whites) who advocate subsuming the struggle against racism within the wider socialist and proletarian struggle against capitalism, and Marxists (mostly blacks) who advocate a specific struggle against racism led by blacks and supported by whites. There is more to this disagreement than a difference of opinion over tactics. It really represents a struggle of its own between two hostile Marxist camps for the hearts and minds of the working class. The advocates of the wider socialist struggle vilify their opponents as black separatists and black vanguardists who are encouraging 'false consciousness' among the proletariat, and playing into the hands of capitalism by dividing the working-class movement. Their opponents retort that the institutional representatives of the wider socialist struggle, the Labour Party and the trade unions, have done nothing to improve the lot of black people, indeed have themselves been implicated in racist policies and racialist practices; and they remain deeply suspicious of what they perceive as moves by left-wing groups to exploit black people's grievances. Gabriel and Ben-Tovim are equally critical of both positions, labelling the former 'a chauvinism of class' and the latter 'a chauvinism of race'; and advocating, instead, an anti-racist struggle which cuts across both race and class and includes non-socialists (Gabriel and Ben-Tovim, 1978). These profound ideological rifts among Marxists and radicals can be detected behind the disagreements over the form and content of anti-racist teaching which I examine towards the end of the next section.

Radicals and Multicultural Education

In this penultimate section I want to take a critical look at the radicals' contribution to the debate about multicultural education. They have addressed themselves to four major issues: the position of ethnic minority or, more often, black children within the education system; the response of the education system to their presence; multicultural education in the normative sense of a set of prescribed policies; and the radical policies to be added, or preferred, to multicultural education in this sense.

1 Underachievement

Assuming that my sketch of radicalism is reasonably accurate, I think it is fair to conclude that it would be in its ideological interests if the defining hallmarks of the ethnic minority experience of British education were underachievement and alienation, with the explanation for both unequivocally identifiable in the ubiquity of racist beliefs and racialist practices. Unfortunately for radicals, such facts as there are (and there exist crucial gaps in the empirical data) either conflict with one another, or point in the opposite direction. For instance, little is known about how Chinese, Cypriot, Irish, Italian or Jewish children fare at school; while much of the research on the scholastic achievements of black children — South Asians and West Indians — is obsolete, small-scale or in other respects unreliable. One fact, however, which does stand out (from, most recently, the evidence collected by the Rampton Committee) is the sharp contrast between the performance of the two black groups in public examinations at 16+ and 18+ — so sharp, indeed, that whether the term 'blacks' should continue to include South Asians has become an unresolved ambiguity in radical discourse. Whereas the attainment profile of South Asians corresponds very closely to that of other pupils in the local authorities where they go to school, and to that of the English school population as a whole, West Indians as a group do conspicuously worse (DES, 1981).

The nature, scale and explanation of West Indian underachievement (and, to a lesser degree, of Asian success) have proved matters of enduring controversy, a veritable forcing-house for ideological growth and dispute. Several commentators on the available research evidence have queried whether the categories employed — 'West Indian' and 'South Asian' — might not be too broad to be really instructive, since they take no account of island origin in the case of the former or national origin in the case of the latter; nor are they normally divided by sex or social class, even though both these factors have long been known to have considerable bearing on children's experience of school. Hence, it could, indeed has been, argued that the relative success of South Asians and the relative failure of West Indians should have been predictable in view of the different educational backgrounds and the different employment profiles of these two groups. In other words (a position popular among radical advocates of the wider socialist struggle), what we are faced with in the underachievement of West Indian children, to the extent that it exists, is not black underachievement but *working-class* under-achievement visibly illustrated.

However that may be, the discussion of the causes of West Indian underachievement has certainly been a replication in miniature of the discussion of the causes of working-class underachievement — 'nature' versus 'nurture'; 'deficit' versus 'difference'; 'inadequate' homes versus 'inadequate' schools. Radicals have on the whole plumped for the baleful influence of racism — 'the racialist attitudes and the racist practices in the larger society and in the educational system itself' (Institute of Race Relations, 1980) — as the decisive factor; with particular stress being laid upon prejudices and stereotypes harboured by the teaching profession. There was a time, a decade ago, when this argument possessed a degree of plausibility — low teacher expectations leading to low self-esteem among black pupils leading to low academic attainment. But more recent research by Delroy Louden and Maureen Stone has knocked the central link out of this chain. In Maureen Stone's words, 'The West Indian children's unfavourable view of their teachers' feelings towards them did not correlate with an unfavourable view of themselves' (Stone, 1981, p. 214). In addition to their failure to establish a causal connection between racism and underachievement, or to get any-where near demonstrating precisely how racism in the education system works to black pupils' disadvantage, there are other weak-nesses in the radicals' hypothesis. If racism is the decisive factor, why do South Asian pupils, also presumably its objects, perform so well? And how is the relative success of West Indian girls, indicated by some research, to be explained; or the fact that the differences in attainment among individual West Indians are far greater than the mean differences between them as a group and other groups?

The critical place occupied by West Indian underachievement in the ideological contest over multicultural education was clearly confirmed when a summary of research by Geoffrey Driver was published in *New Society* in January 1980. Driver had examined the 16+ examination results of five multiethnic secondary schools for the period 1975–78, and concluded that West Indian pupils, for the most part, did better than their English peers (but worse than South Asians); that in some cases West Indians actually overtook English pupils during the course of their secondary school careers; and that West Indian girls did better on average than West Indian boys. These findings generated lively correspondence in subsequent issues of *New Society* and considerable interest nationally. While most correspondents restricted their attention to the validity or otherwise of Driver's data and the conclusions drawn from them, a few were more concerned with the use to which they might be put. One, Colin Prescod, visited his wrath upon the ideological basis to Driver's article and its optimistic liberalism; and upon the anthropologically inspired hypothesis that differences in examination scores between and within ethnic groups could be explained in terms of cultural strength (for example, that West Indian girls tended to do better than West Indian boys because they had been brought up to believe that the future of any family they raised would depend on their social and economic performance not the father's):

> ... [Geoffrey Driver's] piece turned out to be one of wishful thinking, passing as social analysis. There is a breed of latter-day witch-doctors of philosophy abroad, who in spite of their failure to diagnose the ills of the society, feel obligated to promise remedies. They attempt to appease us with incantations and mumbo-jumbo, while passing out placebos.... Britain is patently a class society and a racist society. The postwar experience of expanded numbers of working class black people in Britain is structured by the combined practices related to these ideologies. Unless and until a way is found to fundamentally transform or eradicate these political economic practices, the essential condition of Britain's black population will continue to be an oppressed and exploited one. A significant consequence of this structured reality is that the educational system, which services

and reflects relations in the society, has consistently failed alarming numbers of black children. Some black children, by hook or by crook, as well as by the deliberate but limited intention of the system, do better, academically, than the mass ... only an anti-racism combined with an 'anti-classism' can effectively combat or remove the inequalities which affect [black people's] lives.... (*op. cit.*)

If Driver's article is an expression of optimistic liberalism, then Prescod's letter is an almost perfect epitome of Marxist radicalism, or at any rate of one variant of Marxist radicalism — the significance ascribed to 'base' (what Prescod calls 'structured reality'); the determinist-functionalist view of the relationship between the education system ('services and reflects') and society; and the conviction that short of the revolution little if anything can ever change for the better. Also noteworthy are the radical bent for conspiracy theory (the education system deliberately allowing some, but only some, black children to succeed); the reverence for ideological soundness at the expense of considerations of empirical accuracy (reading between the lines one has the impression that Driver cannot, must not, be right, because if he is the notion of Britain as a deeply 'classist' and racist society begins to look shaky); and the special opprobrium reserved by radicals for anthropologists and cultural explanations ('witch-doctors of philosophy' appeasing us 'with incantations and mumbo-jumbo').*

The fact that the available empirical data do not exactly suit their case (black pupils are no more an educational underclass than their parents are an economic one) has not discouraged radicals, or others, from dealing in generalized assertions about the underachievement of ethnic minority children. Nor has it forestalled the emergence of their alienation hypothesis — that a racist education system is bound to produce a 'culture of resistance' among black pupils. During the 1960s and 1970s several sociologists (for example, Hargreaves, 1967; Lacey, 1970) described the development of anti-school subcultures among working-class pupils in the secondary school. In 1977 this tradition of enquiry was given a dexterous Marxist twist by Paul

---

* For Driver's article, Prescod's letter and other correspondence, see *New Society*, 17 January 1980 and subsequent issues. The complete report of Driver's research was published later in the year (Driver, 1980). A sustained critique, undertaken on behalf of the Rampton Committee, appeared the following year (Taylor, 1981, pp. 113–22).

Willis, whose study of twelve white working-class boys in the Midlands attempted to establish a functional connection between their school experience and the demands of the capitalist economy. Incidental to the main object of his investigation, he also observed the appearance of a pronounced anti-school culture among West Indians in inner city schools: 'We are facing for the first time in this society the possibility of the rejection of contemporary forms and structures of work by at least a significant minority of our second generation immigrant population' (Willis, 1977, p. 85). Three years previously Farrukh Dhondy had offered a similar Marxist analysis in an influential polemic entitled 'The black explosion in schools', published by *Race Today*. He discerned an 'active rebellion' of working-class pupils in schools that, in the case of blacks, amounted to 'nothing less than a crisis of schooling'. He interpreted their indiscipline and rejection of school values not only as a reaction to school as such, but as part of a coordinated resistance to white society's efforts to 'process' or 'deskill' them for the labour market: 'Their [i.e., black pupils'] models of ambition don't include the work ethic ... they challenge discipline, study and routine ... they are the breed most dangerous to capital as they refuse to enter the productive partnership under the terms that this society lays down.' In other words, their school failure was wilful (Dhondy, 1974).

The 'culture of resistance' thesis invites a number of critical comments. First of all, it is rarely clear precisely how grave or extensive the resistance is. One gets the impression from Dhondy's article, for example, that he is really talking about West Indians, not about South Asians, and about boys, not about girls. Secondly, 'resistance' tends to be understood exclusively in terms of open defiance and indiscipline, and to confuse hostility to teachers with hostility to formal education as a whole. In her study of black girls in a London comprehensive school, Mary Fuller comments on the lack of attention paid to the experiences and responses of girls by the 'culture of resistance' thesis, and emphasizes the way those in her sample managed to combine a carefully controlled measure of indiscipline with determination to succeed educationally and economically (Fuller, 1980). Thirdly, the thesis poses interpretation difficulties. To the extent that an 'active rebellion' or 'culture of resistance' can be discerned among black pupils, is it anything other than a visible manifestation of working-class revolt, or indeed of a general adolescent tendency to rebel? Willis concedes not only that the non-conformists at the school he studied were in the minority, but also that 'all schools of whatever class always create oppositional cultures' (Willis, *op. cit*, p. 58). Finally, one is left, by both Dhondy and Willis, with the suspicion that they are actually enamoured, even grudgingly envious, of the rebellious boys they describe — as the vanguard of the revolution perhaps — notwithstanding, in Willis's case, the rebarbative characteristics of *machismo* which vitiate the boys' oppositional culture: racism, sexism and the cult of physical violence.

2　The Response of Education

The differing analyses and critiques presented by radicals in respect of the second and third issues to have occupied their attention — the response of the education system to the presence of ethnic minority pupils, and the development of multicultural education policies — are a product, predictably enough, of their disagreements over 'base' and 'superstructure'; and of how they sort out the relationship between the three key variables they identify — racism, the education system, and the requirements of capitalism. On the one hand, there are the functionalists and determinists who argue that, since racial exploitation and injustice continue to serve the needs of contemporary capitalism, the state's education system will inevitably be permeated with racism, as also will innovations in multicultural education initiated at the state's behest or with its support; genuine reform can only be secured through revolutionary struggle. On the óther hand, there are those who take an interactive view of the relationship between 'base' and 'superstructure', and concede considerable independence to the latter, who argue that, although racism may well have served capitalism's interests in the era of slavery and empire, it has since acquired a momentum of its own that fulfils no clear economic purpose and might even be economically dysfunctional because of the social disruption and division it causes; influential in education racism undoubtedly remains, but more as a cultural legacy of colonialism haunting the collective unconscious, and therefore vulnerable to coherent anti-racist policies mounted from within the system as well as without.

A good example of the functionalist-determinist position is Chris Mullard's paper, 'Racism in Society and Schools', published in 1980. This is how he expresses the relationship between racism, the education system and the requirements of capitalism:

> Racism is not only a permanent, structural, ideological, and
> political feature of British society, but it is also a permanent
> feature of our educational system and of our schools in
> particular.... Not only is the history of mass Church-state
> education a history of the cultural demands of a capitalism
> increasingly dependent upon technological innovation for a
> more 'educated' and thus exploitable labour force, but it is
> also a history of the cultural transmission of ruling class
> ideology.... It is a history concerned with as much the
> stability of Empire as with the stability of the domestic social
> order. (Mullard, 1980, p. 3, 12)

What we have here is the same brand of Marxist radicalism (the
uncharitable might call it 'vulgar') as in Colin Prescod's letter, not
just in its functionalist-determinism (somewhat oddly Mullard com-
bines this with a belief in the 'relative autonomy' of racism 'as an
ideology'), but also in the reliance on unfalsifiable assertion (even in
this context 'permanent' sounds like an overstatement) and conspiracy theory. It comes as no surprise, therefore, to find Mullard
lambasting the educational response to ethnic minorities and multicultural education in an undifferentiated way, and almost as though
they were the same thing:

> Multicultural education not only tends to be conceived within
> a dominant and racist tradition but, perhaps even more
> importantly ... the assumptions on which it appears to be
> based tend ... to legitimise such a tradition and possess the
> effect of containing black resistance.... [Multicultural educa-
> tion] evolved neither as an educational response to the needs
> of black pupils in white schools, nor as a positive response to
> the upsurge of racist events between 1958–1963. But, instead,
> it evolved out of a series of political interpretations made
> about the threat blacks posed to the stability of liberal
> democratic and capitalist society. (Mullard, *op. cit.*, pp. 3–4,
> 15)

Insofar as these assertions have an empirical anchorage, it is an
unsteady one. Mullard's paper repeats two old *canards*, frequently
peddled by radicals in recent years, about government response in the
1960s: that it was assimilationist, and that it located the nature of the
educational problem exclusively in the immigrant children themselves. Ironically, the original source for these criticisms was the
judgement of an essentially liberal research report, *Colour and
Citizenship*, published in 1969:

> The main policy issue defined in the earlier period, 1963–5, was the problem created by the numbers of immigrants entering the schools. The policymakers' main concern was to minimize disturbance to the normal (i.e. the previous) routine of the class or school. They expressed fear lest the class teachers would devote too much time to immigrants at the expense of non-immigrant pupils. The school's role in the process of integration was seen as a social one: it would train immigrants to be British, and provide a location where they could mix with English children. (Rose, *et al.*, 1969, p. 287)

This judicious if sharp assessment, written soon after the period discussed, seems to me substantially correct, but one phrase, 'train immigrants to be British', might, with the benefit of hindsight, have been less ambiguously expressed. Integrationist policy in the 1960s naturally expected schools to help immigrant children adjust to life in Britain, but most emphatically *not*, as many unfamiliar with the period have mistakenly deduced, to encourage them to renounce their ethnic identities in favour of British values. Confusion over this phrase in the *Colour and Citizenship* report has been compounded by widespread misinterpretation of a well-known statement in the second CIAC report of 1964: a national system of education, it reads, 'cannot be expected to perpetuate the different values of immigrant groups' (Home Office, 1964, p. 5). In the context of the whole report, and the other policy documents roughly contemporary with it, this statement simply means that a national system of education cannot be expected to teach Muslim children to be good Muslims or Sikh children to be good Sikhs. Yet, with scant regard for logic, it has been almost universally construed as urging that schools should teach children from the ethnic minorities to become culturally British. Government policy in the 1960s, as distinct from schoolteacher opinion, was never assimilationist in this sense; indeed assimilationism as an aim (as opposed to integrationism) was quite specifically excluded. No more did government policy stereotype immigrant children as problems, or restrict the nature of the educational difficulties to be addressed to those created by their presence. Of course, in a very real way they *were* problems, insofar as they arrived in large numbers over a short period of time, and often from poor, uneducated, rural backgrounds, speaking little or no English or a form of English radically different from that spoken in Britain. But the claim that government policy exclusively defined immigrant children as a problem, even *the* problem, is a fiction which can only be sustained by exaggerating the significance of dispersal policy (quickly discarded, and only ever taken up by a minority of multiethnic authorities), and ignoring what those early official documents had to say about, for example, immigrant children as a resource for curriculum enrichment and the need to counter prejudice and promote enlightened attitudes among the native population.

3   Multicultural Education

Mullard's characterization of multicultural education is equally a caricature. Two features stand out. The first is the pretence that multicultural education is some kind of monolithic entity, incorporating everything from government policy recommendations to expressions of opinion among schoolteachers — including some, those described by Jennifer Williams as part of the Rex and Moore Sparkbrook research of the mid-1960s (Mullard, *op. cit.*, p. 16), with which no advocate of multicultural education would ever identify. Multicultural education has never existed in that sense. This is not to say, as I indicated at the beginning of this chapter, that it has not possessed a certain unity or provided a focus for concern among a number of constituencies — schoolteachers, teacher trainers, researchers and administrators; rather, that it has always been a broad church, accommodating a range of political and educational creeds. Contrary to what Mullard says, multicultural education *did* '[evolve] as an educational response to the needs of black pupils'. To the extent that the movement among teachers began anywhere, it began in the Midlands in the mid-1960s with the formation of ATEPO (the Association for the Teaching of English to — later, for the Education of — Pupils from Overseas), which eventually in the 1970s became the influential national organization NAME (the National Association for Multiracial Education). The second feature of Mullard's caricatured portrait is its cynical interpretation of human motives. The claim that multicultural education is a calculated exercise in social control, defusing black resistance, places his analysis firmly within that tradition of Marxist thought for which all apparently liberal interventions by the state under capitalism (including even race relations legislation) are fundamentally malevolent. There is very little one can retort to assertions of this kind since they seem to have no empirical basis in real life, except perhaps to note Ben-Tovim and Gabriel's wry comment in a different context in regard to race relations legislation: 'If capitalism somehow requires this legislation, then one might expect to find its representatives and not their opponents instrumental in drawing it up' (Ben-Tovim and Gabriel, 1979).

By no means all radicals interpret multicultural education as an exercise in social control on the part of the state. But most remain severely critical of its performance. A common criticism is that it fails to confront racial injustice in the education system and the wider society, being preoccupied instead with cosmetic changes, curriculum tinkering, and diversionary issues such as culture, identity and self-concept. In Maureen Stone's words, 'The reality for most black children is that they are meant for a wageless existence or low wages in unpopular or menial jobs. What has MRE [multiracial education] to say to this fact?' (Stone, *op. cit.*, p. 101). She even goes so far as to implicate multicultural education in black underachievement, arguing, on the basis of the teaching she observed in London schools, that it has taken teachers away from their proper role of imparting knowledge and skills to dabble in social work and psychotherapy. The Institute of Race Relations in its 1980 submission to the Rampton Committee, characterized multicultural education as a manifestation of the 'cultural approach' (labelled 'ethnicism' by Chris Mullard) which so incensed Colin Prescod in Geoffrey Driver's research: 'an ethnic or cultural approach to the educational needs and attainments of racial minorities evades the fundamental reasons for their disabilities — which are the racialist attitudes and the racist practices in the larger society and in the educational system itself' (IRR, 1980, *op cit.*).

4   Radical Alternatives

This brings us to the fourth, and final, major topic to have engaged, and divided, radical opinion — the policies to be added, or preferred, to multicultural education. Maureen Stone is emphatic. Taking Gramsci as her text, she insists that teachers must revert to their socially sanctioned task of imparting necessary knowledge and skills, exchanging child-centred methods for more formal ones: 'only by mastering the traditional curricula will more West Indian children have that basis of choice which many middle-class people take for granted' (Stone, *op. cit.*, pp. 251–2). She can be faulted, like Chris Mullard, for caricaturing multicultural education, and for overstating a case that would not have looked out of place in the conservative Black Papers on education of a decade ago. But there can be little doubt that she speaks for many, maybe most, black parents — and many white ones too — which can hardly be said for other radicals, and certainly not for Farrukh Dhondy. In a second article in *Race Today* published in 1978, four years after 'The black explosion in schools', he developed the black vanguardism of the first. Rejecting the movement for multicultural education, by then well-established in London, in favour of the 'active support from teachers for the independent movement of black people', he argued:

> If I, as a teacher, want to represent black culture ... I am determined to start from the fact that young blacks fight the police, they refuse dirty jobs; their forms of culture gathering always bring them into conflict with the rulers of this society; their very music, professed philosophies and life-styles, contain in them an antagonism to school and to society as it is.... As a teacher I don't want to contain indiscipline, I want to do away with the system that causes it. In the classroom I don't merely want to wear my anti-Nazi badge to prove that I am on the side of the pupils who know that I am paid for processing them. I want instead to work towards developing the power and the alliance that will defeat that processing. I don't want as a teacher to write into my curriculum a chapter about Indian history.... I would rather represent ... the strengths of the black population and try and inculcate in the white pupils of my multi-ethnic classroom a respect of those strengths. (Dhondy, 1978)

This revolutionary programme locates Dhondy's position within the second of the two Marxist anti-racist camps identified by Gabriel and Ben-Tovim, i.e., the advocates of a specific struggle against racism, led by blacks and supported by whites. Joining him there, but advancing a rather different programme, is the Institute of Race Relations. In its submission to the Rampton Committee, the Institute announced that it was working on the production of anti-racist materials 'which will radically re-examine white society and history in the light of the black experience', and help both black and white children 'to develop a critical judgement, not only of their own beliefs and values, but of contemporary social institutions, prevailing attitudes, orthodoxies past and present, and their interrelationship with the actual structure of society.' It was clear from the submission that these materials would have a Marxist orientation (although this was not a label the Institute applied itself) since they would show 'that racialism, like most cultural phenomena, is the concomitant of a particular economic system, which received its main and most sustained impetus in the historical period of colonialism' (IRR, 1980, *op. cit.*). They were published two years later in the form of two readable and attractively presented booklets, *Roots of Racism* and *Patterns of Racism*, designed for secondary school use.

Essentially, these booklets constitute an historical survey of relationships between blacks and whites from a Marxist and black vanguardist point of view, reducing the complex and multifaceted stories of colonialism, imperialism and the transatlantic slave trade to white oppression and black resistance, and to simple economistic explanations and conspiracy theories. For example, the causes of the American Civil War have, in the words of the Marxist historian, E.J. Hobsbawm, been the subject of 'endless dispute among historians'. This is not the impression conveyed by the IRR's account. Its few paragraphs on the war suggest that a single, perfectly straightforward explanation exists — economic competition between North and South. Interestingly, this explanation does not tally with Hobsbawm's. 'In purely economic terms', he writes, 'the North was not much worried about the South' (Hobsbawm, 1977, pp. 170–3). Whatever the truth of the matter, the main point is that, whereas modern developments in history teaching are in the direction of helping children to master the disciplinary skills of sifting and evaluating historical evidence, the Institute of Race Relations has reverted to the reactionary pedagogy of trying to impose upon them a single version of events. At its worst, this degenerates into potted history of the crudest kind:

> Throughout the centuries of imperialism, writers and scholars worked to 'prove' the theories of racism, to make them respectable and put them beyond doubt. Hitler's theories of the racial superiority of the German people were developed directly from these earlier thinkers, and his attempt to wipe the Jews and Gypsies off the face of the earth was their logical conclusion. (IRR, 1982, p. 39)

A re-reading ought to have suggested, even to subscribers to conspiracy theory, that 'logical conclusion' was hardly the most appropriate phrase.

The best known exponent, in the field of education, of the other Marxist anti-racist school of thought identified by Gabriel and Ben-Tovim (the advocates of the wider socialist struggle) is Chris Searle. In the introduction to his compilation of writing from an East End secondary school, *The World in a Classroom*, he stakes out a Marxist position on the relationship between schools and society which manages to combine determinist-functionalism with an almost utopian faith in what socialist teachers can achieve through the system:

> ... under capitalism, the school is a Janus. It is the institution of a State which condones the exploitation of an entire class, and promotes racism to divide its greatest enemy — which is that same class — for its own economic interest and survival. It is a part of the apparatus which seeks to provide a semi-literate and compliant labour force to man industry and public services. It turns out black and immigrant labour to perform some of the dirtiest, most tedious and badly-paid jobs in society. And yet within the school, which, as an institution of the State may purposefully underdevelop black and white working class minds, there is a growing power of resistance and commitment to transform the State and the school as a servant institution of the State.... The school may ultimately serve the State, but it holds within it forces that can contribute to transforming the State.... For a teacher who is committed to the socialist transformation of society, and the transformation of the nature of the School itself, the classroom is a vital powerhouse. The teacher uses the cracks and contradictions of the school to deliver continuous body-blows to its function under capitalism.... The school, transformed and moved towards becoming a workshop of struggle, is potentially one of our strongest weapons and bulwarks against racism. (Searle, 1977, pp. 13–15)

The outcome of the 'workshop of struggle' created by Searle and his colleagues was an integrated curriculum course for second and third year pupils drawing on topical events in the East End and its 'anti-fascist' history; the children's own experiences; and stories of oppression and resistance in the Third World. The aim was partly to expose racist myths and stereotypes, and to provide a vigorous challenge to the racialist activities of the right-wing groups who had at that time secured some political purchase on white working-class attitudes in the East End. But, in addition (and more significantly), it aimed to forge a new internationally-based sense of solidarity among the children — laying the foundations perhaps for a new proletarian hegemony — in which race and colour consciousness would be replaced by, or at any rate be subordinated to, class consciousness. For this Searle claims a degree of success: 'The children were not slow to recognise that it was their class that ultimately united them with other oppressed people all over the world and not necessarily their colour' (Searle, *op. cit.*, p. 97). Obviously one is at the mercy of Searle's judgement here. Where one is not, however, is in recognizing the outstanding quality of the children's writing — autobiographies, playlets, poems, stories — produced as part of the course and of which *The World in a Classroom* largely consists. Herein lies much of the explanation for the paradox of Searle's popularity in liberal educational circles. The emphasis given to children's personal writing in his pedagogy, and the methods used to inspire it, place him unmistakeably in the Romantic tradition of creativity which I identified earlier as one of liberalism's three main ideological tributaries. There is another reason, for his popularity. His integrationist internationalism, despite its overtly Marxist complexion, does not really seem so very different from the liberal integrationism of the 1960s; 'the world in a classroom' is merely another way of expressing the 1964 CIAC report's idealized notion of the multiracial school as a microcosm of a harmonious multiracial community.

Anti-racist teaching comes, of course, in as many shapes and sizes as multicultural education. Some anti-racists claim to be multi-culturalists as well (and *vice versa*), and they would probably want to distance themselves from at least one of the three representatives of anti-racist strategy I have elected to concentrate upon in this section. For my purposes, the advantage of examining their work is that it vividly highlights, at the level of school or classroom practice, the sharp divorce between Marxist radicalism and liberalism, since all three, in their different ways, propose a model of teaching and learning which is indoctrinatory, and therefore illiberal, in character. Dhondy unashamedly uses the word 'inculcate', and Searle makes no bones about the fact that he is teaching his pupils to be socialists. Only the Institute of Race Relations is more devious. Its submission to the Rampton Committee speaks of developing 'critical judgement'; but it is evident from *Roots of Racism* and *Patterns of Racism* that this does not mean, as it would for a liberal, developing children's critical faculties so that they can form their own judgements on a rational basis. It means teaching them to be critical (in the narrower negative sense) of capitalism and of its 'products' in the 'superstructure'.

End Note

All writers about ideology are under an obligation to make plain their own ideological attachment. My own attachment to liberalism has, I hope, always been plain enough (Jeffcoate, 1977, 1979); and this chapter should have proved no exception. This does not mean that I am unaware of liberalism's weaknesses. Marxist strictures are not without point: liberalism does lack theoretical rigour; and it has been shown up, all too often, as naively optimistic. Nor does it mean that I am unimpressed or uninfluenced by Marxist analysis, or that I am wholly hostile to the Marxist educationists discussed here. I have long been an admirer of Chris Searle's work (but not his prose), and nurse a secret sympathy for Maureen Stone's rather reactionary position; and the warmth and humour of Farrukh Dhondy's school stories (*East End at Your Feet, Come to Mecca*) suggest that he is not really the big bad wolf he would have us believe. However, the Marxist approach to education remains inferior to liberalism in two crucial respects: evidence and practice. It has been consistently cavalier in its treatment of empirical data, using its theoretical ingenuity to squirm out of tight corners when the facts do not fit (for an excellent critique of the Marxist approach to education, see Hickox, 1982); and it has yet to explain how its own recommendations for school and teacher practice are to be distinguished from indoctrination, if indeed they are. Yet Marxists and radicals have so far had things very much their own way in the critical analysis of multicultural education. This chapter is intended as a liberal response.

References

BEN-TOVIM, G. and GABRIEL, J. (1979) 'The politics of race in Britain 1962–79: A review of the major trends and of recent debates', *Race Relations Abstracts*, Vol. 4.

DES (1981) *West Indian Children in Our Schools*, ('Rampton Report'), London, HMSO.

DHONDY, F. (1974) 'The black explosion in schools', *Race Today*, February.

DHONDY, F. (1978) 'Teaching young blacks', *Race Today*, May/June.

DRIVER, G. (1980) *Beyond Underachievement*, London, Commission for Racial Equality.

ENTWISTLE, H. (1979) *Antonio Gramsci: Conservative Schooling for Radical Politics*, London, Routledge and Kegan Paul.

FULLER, M. (1980) 'Black girls in a London Comprehensive', in DEEM, R. (Ed.), *Schooling for Women's Work*, London, Routledge and Kegan Paul.

GABRIEL, J. and BEN-TOVIM, G. (1978) 'Marxism and the concept of racism', *Economy and Society*, 7, 2.

HARGREAVES, D.H. (1967) *Social Relations in a Secondary School*, London, Routledge and Kegan Paul.

HARGREAVES, D.H. (1982) *The Challenge for the Comprehensive School: Culture, Curriculum and Community*, London, Routledge and Kegan Paul.

HICKOX, M.S.H. (1982) 'The Marxist sociology of education: A critique', *The British Journal of Sociology*, 33, 4.

HOBSBAWM, E.J. (1977) *The Age of Capital 1848–1875*, Abacus.

HOME OFFICE (1964) *Second Report of Commonwealth Immigrants Advisory Council*, Cmnd 2266, London, HMSO.

HOME OFFICE (1981) *The Brixton Disorders 10–12 April 1981*, Cmnd 8427, ('Scarman Report'), London.

INSTITUTE OF RACE RELATIONS (1980) *Anti-Racist Not Multicultural Education*, London, IRR.

INSTITUTE OF RACE RELATIONS (1982) *Roots of Racism; Patterns of Racism*, London, IRR.

JEFFCOATE, R. (1977) 'Schools and racism', *Multiracial School*, 6, 1.

JEFFCOATE, R. (1979) *Positive Image: Towards a Multiracial Curriculum*, Writers and Readers.

LACEY, C. (1970) *Hightown Grammar*, Manchester, Manchester University Press.

MULLARD, C. (1980) *Racism in Society and Schools: History, Policy and Practice*, Centre for Multicultural Education, University of London Institute of Education.

POPPER, K. (1976) *Unended Quest: An Intellectual Autobiography*, Fontana/Collins.

ROSE, E.J.B. *et al.* (1969) *Colour and Citizenship: A Report on British Race Relations*, Institute of Race Relations/Oxford University Press.

STONE, M. (1981) *The Education of the Black Child in Britain*, Fontana.

TAYLOR, M. (1981) *Caught Between: A Review of Research into the Education of Pupils of West Indian Origin*, Windsor, NFER.

WILLIS, P. (1977) *Learning to Labour: How Working Class Kids Get Working Class Jobs*, Farnborough, Saxon House.

Select Bibliography

BANKS, J.A. (1981) *Multi-Ethnic Education: Theory and Practice*, Boston, Mass., Allyn and Bacon.

BANTON, M. (1983) *Racial and Ethnic Competition*, Cambridge, Cambridge University Press.

BARTON, L. and WALKER, S. (Eds) (1983) *Race, Class and Education*, London, Croom Helm.

BHATNAGAR, J. (Ed.) (1981) *Educating Immigrants*, London, Croom Helm.

BULLIVANT, B. (1981) *The Pluralist Dilemma in Education*, Sydney, Allen and Unwin.

COHEN, L. and MANION, L. (1983) *Multicultural Classrooms*, London, Croom Helm.

COLEMAN, D.A. (Ed.) (1982) *Demography of Immigrants and Minority Groups in the U.K.*, Academic Press.

CRAFT, A.Z. and BARDELL, G. (Eds) (1984, forthcoming) *Curriculum Opportunities in a Multicultural Society*, Harper and Row.

CRAFT, M. (Ed.) (1981) *Teaching in a Multicultural Society: The Task for Teacher Education*, Lewes, Falmer Press.

DES (1981) *West Indian Children in Our Schools*, ('Rampton Report'), London, HMSO.

EDWARDS, V. (1983) *Language in Multicultural Classrooms*, Batsford.

GARCIA, R.L. (1982) *Teaching in a Pluralistic Society*, Harper and Row.

GILES, H. and SAINT-JACQUES, B. (1979) *Language and Ethnic Relations*, Oxford, Pergamon.

GLAZER, N. and MOYNIHAN, D.P. (1975) *Ethnicity: Theory and Practice*, Harvard University Press.

HOULTON, D. and WILLEY, R. (1983) *Supporting Children's Bilingualism*, Longman Resources Unit for the Schools Council.

HOUSE OF COMMONS (1981) *Racial Disadvantage*. Fifth Report of the Home Affairs Committee, London, HMSO.

JAMES, A. and JEFFCOATE, R. (Eds) (1981) *The School in the Multicultural Society*, Harper and Row.

KLEIN, G. (1982) *Resources for Multicultural Education: An Introduction*, Longman Resources Unit for the Schools Council.

KREJCI, J. and VELIMSKY, V. (1981) *Ethnic and Political Nations in Europe*, London, Croom Helm.

LYNCH, J. (1983) *The Multicultural Curriculum*, Batsford.

MILLER, J. (1983) *Many Voices: Bilingualism, Culture and Education*, London, Routledge and Kegan Paul.

MILNER, D. (1983) *Children and Race Ten Years On*, Ward Lock.

MUSGROVE, F. (1982) *Education and Anthropology*, Chichester, Wiley.

NANN, R. (Ed.) (1982) *Uprooting and Surviving*, Reidel.

NEWMAN, W.M. (1973) *American Pluralism: Minority Groups and Social Theory*, Harper and Row.

OPEN UNIVERSITY (1982) *Ethnic Minorities and Community Relations*, (Course E354), Open University Press.

RAMIREZ, M. and CASTANADA, A. (1974) *Cultural Democracy, Bicognitive Development and Education*, Academic Press.

REX, J. (1983) *Race Relations in Sociological Theory*, London, Routledge and Kegan Paul.

ROSEN H. and BURGESS, T. (1981) *Languages and Dialects of London Schoolchildren*, Ward Lock.

RUNNYMEDE TRUST (1980) *Britain's Black Population*, Heinemann.

SAID, A.A. and SIMMONS, L.R. (Eds) (1976) *Ethnicity in an International Context*, New Jersey, Transaction Books.

SMOLICZ, J.J. (1979) *Culture and Education in a Plural Society*, Canberra, Curriculum Development Centre.

STONE, M. (1981) *The Education of the Black Child in Britain*, Fontana.

TOMLINSON, S. (1983) *Ethnic Minorities in British Schools: A Review of the Literature*, Heinemann.

TOMLINSON, S. (1984, forthcoming) *Home and School in Multicultural Britain*, Batsford.

UNESCO (1982) *Living in Two Cultures*, Gower.

VERMA, G.K. and BAGLEY, C. (Eds) (1979) *Race, Education and Identity*, London, Macmillan.

WATSON, J.L. (Ed.) (1977) *Between Two Cultures*, Oxford, Blackwell.

Notes on Contributors

MAURICE CRAFT is Professor of Education and Pro-Vice-Chancellor at Nottingham University, where he is Chairman of the School of Education. Director of the national 'Training the Trainers' programme in multicultural education, his publications include *Teaching in a Multicultural Society (1981)* and (with Madeleine Atkins) *Training Teachers of Ethnic Minority Community Languages* (1983).

VIV EDWARDS is a lecturer in applied linguistics at Birkbeck College, University of London, and is also currently co-director of the SSRC project on 'Patterns of Language Use in British Black Adolescents'. Her main publications include *The West Indian Language Issue in British Schools* (1979) and *Language in Multicultural Classrooms* (1983).

PETER FIGUEROA, lecturer in education and Chairman of the Centre for International Studies in Education at Southampton University, has lectured at the Universities of the West Indies, Frankfurt and Dar-es-Salaam, and is Chairman of the Association of African, Caribbean and Asian Academics. His publications include *Sociology of Education: A Caribbean Reader* (1976).

ROBERT JEFFCOATE was Development Officer on the Schools Council project, 'Education for a Multiracial Society', and until recently a lecturer in educational studies at The Open University and a member of the course team in multicultural education. He is the author of *Positive Image* (1979), and of a number of articles on multicultural education.

THE LINGUISTIC MINORITIES PROJECT, directed by Dr Verity Saifullah Khan, was a DES-funded research project based at London University Institute of Education from 1979 to 1983. Its overall aim has been to provide an account and analysis of the bilingualism of ethnic minorities in England, and to contribute to the development of policy on language education.

JAMES LYNCH is Professor of Education, Head of Teaching Studies, and Dean of the Faculty of Education at Sunderland Polytechnic. He has worked in teacher education in the UK and overseas, and is a consultant to national and international organizations. His publications include *Teaching in the Multicultural School* (1981) and *The Multicultural Curriculum* (1983).

KEN THOMAS is a lecturer in the social psychology of education at Nottingham University. His current research interests focus on the influence of race on children's social relationships, and he has jointly directed the Schools Council 'Lifestyles' project at Nottingham University which has developed materials to sensitize teachers to the implications of cultural diversity.

SALLY TOMLINSON is a senior lecturer in the Department of Educational Research at Lancaster University, where she teaches and researches in race and education, and in special education. Her publications include *Colonial Immigrants in a British City* (1979), with John Rex, and *Ethnic Minorities in British Schools: A Review of the Literature* (1983).

RICHARD WILLEY is a freelance writer on education whose recent publications include *Multi-ethnic Education: The Way Forward* (1981), with Alan Little; *Teaching in Multicultural Britain* (1982); *Studies in the Multi-Ethnic Curriculum* (1983), with Alan Little; and *Multicultural Britain: The Preparation of Teachers* (1983), for the CRE Advisory Group on Teacher Education.

Index

Index

Index